The LIBRARY INNOVATION TOOLKIT

Ideas, Strategies, and Programs

Edited by Anthony Molaro
and Leah L. White

Foreword by R. David Lankes

AN IMPRINT OF THE AMERICAN LIBRARY ASSOCIATION
CHICAGO 2015

© 2015 by the American Library Association

Extensive effort has gone into ensuring the reliability of the information in this book; however, the publisher makes no warranty, express or implied, with respect to the material contained herein.

ISBNs
978-0-8389-1274-4 (paper)
978-0-8389-1258-4 (PDF)
978-0-8389-1259-1 (ePub)
978-0-8389-1260-7 (Kindle)

Library of Congress Cataloging-in-Publication Data
The library innovation toolkit : ideas, strategies, and programs / edited by Anthony Molaro and Leah L. White ; foreword by R. David Lankes.
    pages cm
  Includes bibliographical references and index.
  ISBN 978-0-8389-1274-4
 1. Library administration. 2. Organizational change. 3. Libraries and community. 4. Public services (Libraries) 5. Libraries—Activity programs. 6. Libraries—Technological innovations. 7. Library administration—United States—Case studies. I. Molaro, Anthony, editor. II. White, Leah L., editor.
  Z678.L463 2015
  025.1—dc23
                          2014038864

Cover Design by Krista Joy Johnson. Images © Shutterstock.
Book design and composition in the Chaparral Pro, Boudoir, and Edmondsans typefaces by Ryan Scheife / Mayfly Design.

♾ This paper meets the requirements of ANSI/NISO Z39.48–1992 (Permanence of Paper).

Printed in the United States of America

19 18 17 16 15   5 4 3 2 1

The LIBRARY
INNOVATION
TOOLKIT

CONTENTS

Part I   Innovative Culture

Part II   Innovative Staff

FOREWORD

R. David Lankes

Nothing is different, but everything's changed.

—Paul Simon and Brian Eno
"Once Upon a Time There Was an Ocean"

I recently took a family vacation to Walt Disney World. There, in the Magic Kingdom's Tomorrowland is a ride called the Carousel of Progress. It is a rotating stage show that follows an animatronic family as it copes with progress (mostly technological advancements) at the turn of the twentieth century, in the 1920s, 1940s, and sort of today (more like the 1990s). The theme throughout each tableau is the same: look how far we've come; we live in a great era of innovation.

What is interesting about the ride/show is that each era makes a claim that its time is the era of great progress and innovation. "Look, indoor plumbing—how could it get any better?" "Look, electricity—surely we are living in the greatest time of advancement." "Look, a stove that is voice activated—there's a great big beautiful tomorrow...." It is a trap that we all often fall into when we describe innovation and advancements in our own era. It is a narrative that we adopt and is clear throughout this book: this is a time of great change and, in implication, the era of greatest change.

My point is not to challenge this concept—it is clear we are in a time of great change—but rather to say that it is a narrative we adopt, and often from previous generations. We are, as a society and as a field, addicted to innovation. Those who talk about librarianship as a risk-averse, slow-moving field have not been paying attention. Adoption of social networking and makerspaces has come on the heels of adoption of virtual reference, which came upon adoption of the Internet itself, after the adoption of the personal computer, after the adoption of microfiche. Michael Gorman once referred to the library as the graveyard of abandoned technologies.

True innovation is not simply change that matches this larger societal meme of progress for progress's sake. True innovation is positive change, and when you assign terms like *positive* or *negative*, you must have some standard to measure it against. Positive for whom? Compared to what? At what cost? As Walt Disney's script calls out the miracles of electricity and cars, he does not talk about (nor was he likely aware of) the environmental impact of pollution and greenhouse gases. He talks about commuting and the rise of suburbs without mentioning the ensuing urban blight.

So, how can we look, not just at change, but at innovation—positive change? I believe the answer is put succinctly by Hashemi Scott and McNamee in chapter 1 of this book: "Libraries serve communities, and communities change."

I might add that libraries are part of those served communities as well. As the condition of communities improves, so should the condition of the libraries and librarians. My point is that it is the community that must be our yardstick and arbiter for good and bad—not the collection (making it bigger, making it circulate more, making it better described), but the community and the community's ability to fulfill its needs *and* aspirations. And, as Hashemi Scott and McNamee note, these needs and aspirations change, and so must libraries and librarians—change, not to fit a narrative, but to improve their communities and society as a whole.

This book adds to the conversation around innovation and change going on in librarianship but also, and more important, at the interface between librarians and communities. I see each chapter as a sort of case study. These cases serve as necessary reality to more conceptual discussions on innovation and the predominant narrative that innovation is good because change is good. These chapters, however, call out for the next step, the next turn of the conversation: making cases transferrable and assessable across libraries and, indeed, across domains.

So, I have a request of you, dear reader. As you read this book and you spark upon a good idea, first, do the good idea. Second, reach out to the author behind that idea. Every project I have ever embarked upon improved by sharing. This book is one side of a conversation; add the other side. Link these ideas into your practice, but also deeper concepts and theories. Use these ideas, these points, these work plans as a foundation for a larger personal network of innovation.

To steal from Walt Disney's song: there is a great big beautiful tomorrow shining for libraries and librarians. That tomorrow will come from a coordinated effort to network as professionals, and to include our communities as part of the library, not simply as consumers of ideas we dream up.

ACKNOWLEDGMENTS

TONY'S ACKNOWLEDGMENTS

I wish to thank Lori Donovan, my graduate assistant, who helped me immensely with formatting the following chapters into Chicago style. I also wish to extend my endless gratitude to Leah White, who has been a steadfast partner-in-library-crime with me over the years. I admire your work and continuously look up to you. I also want to thank the faculty, administration, staff, and students of St. Catherine University, MLIS Program, who challenge me, inspire me, and teach me each and every day. Last, I want to thank Erika Molaro, who has been so patient with me while I read, write, edit, and get into projects way over my head.

LEAH'S ACKNOWLEDGMENTS

Few projects happen in a vacuum, and I would like to first thank Dr. Anthony Molaro for being my partner throughout the years on several massive and successful projects...more massive than we often realized. It's hard to find someone who is both a friend and a good partner. You're the tops, Dr. Molaro. I would also like to thank Stefan Moorehead, my partner in life, who keeps me grounded, focused, reading, and also laughing. Finally, a big thank-you to my mentors over the past few years, including Dr. Michael Stephens, Audrey Chapuis, Natalya Fishman, and Eric Robbins, who have all in some way taught me to live and breathe libraries, think creatively, and never give up.

OUR ACKNOWLEDGMENTS

We wish to thank David Lankes for agreeing to write the foreword for this book. As you will see throughout the chapters, his work has inspired and empowered many of the librarians who contributed to this book. We also wish to thank ALA Editions for agreeing to take on this project and working with us to get it done.

INTRODUCTION

Anthony Molaro and Leah L. White

We live in a fascinating time. Sure, there aren't flying cars, but every day something new, exciting, and totally different is launched or announced or, sometimes, declared. The ways we consume and then disseminate information are shifting. The ways people think and interact are transforming. And the way libraries provide services for their communities is rapidly changing.

Innovation seems easy enough. According to the *Merriam-Webster Dictionary* (2014), innovation is "the act or process of introducing new ideas, devices, or methods," and this sounds like a pretty simple concept. In reality and in the day-to-day life of a library worker, trying to innovate can occasionally feel like moving mountains. Yet libraries, despite budget restraints, staffing issues, and all nature of obstacles, continue to innovate in the most fascinating ways in order to fulfill their missions and create positive experiences for their patrons.

Many argue that innovation is not so much a destination as it is a process. We would add that innovation is not a process as much as it is an organizational (or departmental) culture, mind-set, or worldview. Innovation needs to be systematically ingrained in us as librarians and library organizations. It requires a dedication to the innovative spirit, to looking at problems through a holistic lens, to experimentation and rapid prototyping, and to taking risks.

Innovation doesn't always mean a disruption but can also include incremental or sustaining innovations, but in both cases the goal is the same: to offer the best experiences and services for patrons. Again, innovation doesn't need to be a big, shiny, new thing but can also include small tweaks and alterations to existing services, tools, and spaces.

What you will glean from the following chapters is that innovation is much less focused on technology and much more focused on people, either staff or patrons. Innovation happens through people (library staff) to improve services and experiences for the community (patrons). In the chapters of this book lie outstanding and unique examples of ways libraries and librarians are innovating to not only keep up with the times but also lead the way into the future.

Innovative Culture

Part I introduces the innovation mind-set framework. "Zen and the Art of Innovation," by Sarah Hashemi Scott and Heather McNamee, introduces the beginner's mind as a crucial element of innovative cultures. The next chapter, "Driving Creativity and Innovation in Your Organization: It's Easier Than You Think," by Kelly Pepo, discusses the importance of creating organizational structures that lead to innovation. Pepo introduces the concept of Innovation Champions, who are tasked with monitoring trends while seeds committees are tasked with caring for an idea from inception to fruition. This part's concluding chapter, "The Library's Role in Promoting Tolerance and Diversity in a University," by Lorna E. Rourke, shows how innovation can mean standing up for those whose voice is often silenced. Readers will see that to be innovative may require us to be bold and to take great political risks, even in the face of opposition.

Innovative Staff

Part II is devoted to strategies for building staff buy-in for innovative ideas and engagement in innovation practices. This part begins with "Innovation Wizardry," by Sarah Strahl and Erica J. Christianson, which examines the "magical" aspects of innovation as we learn innovative wizardry. "Innovative Boot Camp: A Social Experiment," by Robin Bergart and M. J. D'Elia, walks readers through a systematic, boot camp–style approach to innovation, through which we learn to ask, Why do we do things this way versus that way? The concluding chapter, "Building a Toolkit to Craft Your Instruction

Program: The Virginia Tech Experience," by Tracy M. Hall, Edward F. Lener, and Purdom Lindblad, offers a toolkit to kick-start your instructional program. In each of these chapters, readers will find a step-by-step process for achieving certain innovative outcomes.

Innovative Outreach

Part III is about getting outside the library to deliver exceptional and innovative outreach services to patrons. From catching a ferry across the bay ("Get on Board with Community Needs: Ferry Tales, a Monthly Book Group aboard a Ferry," by Audrey Barbakoff) to grabbing a drink in a bar ("A Librarian Walks into a Bar," by Ben Haines and Kate Niehoff), readers will see the essential role librarians play in expanding the library beyond its own walls. Both chapters talk about the importance of reaching a fuller part of the community, particularly the community that doesn't use the library. We may not all have the luxury of jumping on a ferry, but many of us can apply this type of inventiveness to our own communities in unique and meaningful ways.

Innovative Technology

While both of the chapters in Part IV come to us from academic libraries, they are fully applicable to libraries of all types. The first chapter, "Seizing the Opportunity for Innovation and Service Improvement," by Cheryl McGrath and Brad Warren, provides two examples of using technology to improve the experience of the user. Both projects not only improved user experience, and saved their time, but also saved the library money. In "The 'Eyes' Have It: A Digital Media Lab in an Academic Library," Pat Duck describes the creation and implementation of a digital media lab, providing guidance and examples for any type of institution that may wish to create this much-needed service.

Innovative Spaces

Part V concerns library spaces. Monica Harris's "Participatory Spaces and Idea Box" explores how to create a truly unique participatory space for all patrons. The space inspires the creativity of community members, serves as a way to exhibit their work, and builds anticipation for the next iteration of the idea box. "'Like a Kid in a Candy Store': Marketplaces in Public Libraries," by Daisy Porter-Reynolds, deals with merchandising our collections, and why we don't need to reinvent the wheel when publishers and retailers have figured out all of this stuff with their deep, marketing dollars–lined pockets. This chapter incorporates the best practices of our retailing competition to improve the services for our patrons and provide them with a system with which they are more comfortable.

Innovative Programs

Part VI, the book's longest part, highlights several innovative program ideas. In each of the chapters, readers will find unique ways to create positive experiences for our patrons. From re-envisioning a children's writing club ("Apprentices of the Book Empire at a Glance," by Amy Holcomb and Anna Fillmore), to launching a Readtember (month of literacy) program with zombies, dads, and gaming ("Monsters, Rockets, and Baby Racers: Stepping into the Story with Children and Young People," by Matt Finch and Tracie Mauro), to running a C2E2-style comic convention ("Librari-Con: Bringing Magic to Your Library," by Erika Earp and Melissa Lang), to creating a TED-style event for your community ("The Business of Ideas: Using a TED-Like Event to Spread Innovation," by Troy A. Swanson), the reader will see a common thread emerge. Each of these programs requires an innovative attitude, a willingness to fail and to learn from mistakes, and a deep desire to reach new patrons and create positive experiences for all.

We hope that you enjoy the contents of this book. May it inspire you to take big risks, ask deeper questions, strive for better service, and dream bigger ideas. As Brian Mathews (2012) once remarked, "Innovation is messy. It takes many wild ideas that flop in order to find transformative gold. Innovation demands leaders who are persistent and who can challenge the status quo. Innovation requires organizations to live in liminality. Is your library ready for disruption?" (3).

REFERENCES

Mathews, Brian. 2012. "Think Like a Startup: A White Paper to Inspire Library Entrepreneurialism." VTechWorks. Posted April 3, 2012. http://vtechworks.lib .vt.edu/handle/10919/18649.

Merriam-Webster Dictionary. 2014. S.v. "innovation." Accessed September 29. www.merriam-webster.com/dictionary/innovation.

PART I

INNOVATIVE
CULTURE

1

Zen and the Art of Innovation

Sarah Hashemi Scott and Heather McNamee

Innovation is a hot topic in all industries and service sectors these days. In recent years, innovation has become a central focus of conferences, publishing, research, and popular discourse and has emerged as a key strategic priority in organizations of all kinds, from public sector agencies to large corporations. Innovation, by definition, means change and moving toward the unknown. There is no blueprint. However, putting innovation in its proper context—the rich history of human society—offers us a framework for understanding why it is important, how we can become better innovators, and how libraries can support innovation in society at large.

In this chapter, we argue that success in innovation begins in the mind, and we describe how having the right mind-set will help everyone in your library through the process. We begin by considering why innovation has become a key strategic priority and examining how recent developments in technology have transformed society and culture and placed new pressures and demands upon libraries and other organizations. We also explore the relationship between innovation in libraries and innovation in other sectors, positioning libraries as facilitators of knowledge creation and innovation throughout society and as potential partners in coordinated efforts to improve society. Finally, we describe qualities of the innovative mind-set, drawing on the concept of "beginner's mind" from Zen Buddhism, and offer a number of practical suggestions for both managers and frontline staff to help foster innovation in their own work and organizations.

Background and Context

We live in the Information Age, and our world is rapidly changing. New, disruptive technologies continually emerge, gain widespread adoption throughout society, and impact the ways in which people live, learn, work, communicate, and interact. The past few decades have seen the emergence of the Internet, mobile communication, digital media, blogs, online social networks, and 3-D printing—several examples of technologies that have profoundly changed, and continue to change, the lives of people across the globe. These historic changes of the recent past and present continue to dramatically transform twenty-first-century society, as the Industrial Revolution transformed society in the late eighteenth and early nineteenth centuries. Information and communication platforms such as Twitter and Facebook and technological tools such as smart phones and tablet computers are now available to and utilized by a wider spectrum of society than ever before. The globalization of communication networks, information systems, economies, and workforces has linked people to one another across the world in unprecedented ways, and the advent of the Internet has eradicated many of the geographic and socioeconomic barriers that isolated communities in times past. We live in a world of ubiquitous social connections. In the words of entrepreneur and author Seth Godin (2008): "Geography used to be important....Now, the Internet eliminates geography" (11).

Libraries serve communities, and communities change. As we have seen, geography is no longer a precursor to forming or maintaining a community, and as new communication networks give rise to new communities, people connect to one another in new and different ways. People are more mobile than ever before, and relationships that begin online often develop offline, leading people to move to be with new friends or partners, take new jobs, pursue education, or start new businesses. In addition, political conflicts drive migrations of large populations from one city or country to another. Migrations and circumstances shift the demographics of local communities, which are the traditional types of communities that libraries have focused on serving. This leads to new demands from library users. Innovation becomes a necessity and an explicit strategic priority.

As new communities form and as existing communities change and evolve, values—both inside and outside our organizations—conflict and shift. From democratic uprisings in the Arab world and partisan politics in the United States to the "free knowledge" movement and the shifting balance between traditional publishing and self-publishing, the values and interests of different parties clash and compete and put pressure on libraries and other organizations to adapt. Although the profession of librarianship is grounded in a number of traditional values, including intellectual freedom, privacy, and confidentiality, these values are often challenged by the development of new technologies and services, compelling librarians to prioritize certain values over others or to resist change in light of the ethical dilemmas it presents. Tensions between professional values concerning privacy, preservation, digital access, filtering, and censorship are evident in many areas of our field today, including the delivery of e-books and other digital media to patrons, the provision of public Internet access, and the adoption of social online public access catalogs (OPACs). Internal conflicts over values present barriers to—and opportunities for—innovation.

Approaches to innovation in the private and public sectors vary. The differences lie mainly in motivations. According to Christian Bason (2010), Director of Denmark's innovation unit MindLab, "in the private sector competition and the efficiency of markets is [sic] generally regarded as the main source of innovative pressure," whereas in the public sector innovation is motivated by community needs (61). In democratic nations such as the United States, public sector organizations such as libraries, schools, and city or county agencies operate within the framework of democracy. The purpose of any particular organization can be discerned from many sources, including its formal charter or charge, mission and vision statements, strategic plans, and guiding principles. Public sector organizations are bound by their role in the community to a greater extent than are private sector innovators. For example, Google's approach to innovation is centered on their product, aiming "to take things that work well and improve upon them in unexpected ways" (Google Inc. 2013), whereas the US government's Office of Social Innovation and Civic Participation is tasked with making "greater and more lasting progress on our Nation's challenges" (SICP 2013).

Libraries play a unique role in the ecosystem of innovation. As providers of access to information and as facilitators of the creation of new knowledge, libraries foster innovation throughout society. By being adept at innovation ourselves, we can better meet the needs and demands of the communities we serve, thereby better facilitating innovation throughout society. In addition, in partnership and collaboration with other organizations such as schools and universities, city agencies, or nonprofits, libraries can play an important role in coordinated efforts to address community needs and improve society.

Given the environments in which our organizations operate, the imperative to innovate has taken on a new sense of urgency. So, how is a twenty-first-century library to succeed at innovation? One key step toward success in innovation is to adopt an innovative mind-set. This is something that individuals and organizations can do immediately as they begin their journey toward creating flexible, responsive, and effective organizations. We can learn a lot about the state of mind most conducive to innovation by turning our attention to the school of thought known as Zen Buddhism. In the following sections, we explore beginner's mind concepts from Zen Buddhism as articulated in Shunryu Suzuki's (1997) book *Zen Mind, Beginner's Mind: Informal Talks on Zen Meditation and Practice*, incorporating these with practical applications for both frontline staff and managers in libraries.

The idea that Zen teachings can be applied to innovation is not new. In a 2012 post on Fast Company's design blog *Co.DESIGN*, Warren Berger discussed several recent books linking Zen teachings and innovation. Berger asserted that his own research on the relationship between fundamental questioning and innovation supports the notion that "some of the most successful innovators adopt a 'question everything' mindset that could be compared to the Zen notion of *shoshin*, or 'beginner's mind.'"

Beginner's mind is a state of openness to the point of emptiness. With a beginner's mind one sees things as they are, can hold many possibilities in the mind at once, has no thought of achievement, gives full attention to the present moment, and uses straightforward communication. The beginner's mind is patient and calm: "in the midst of noise and change, your mind will be quiet and stable" (Suzuki 1997, 57–58). The qualities of an innovative mind-set discussed in this chapter are organized under broad categories: Communication, Perception, and Action. Each quality is discussed with an eye toward practical applications for frontline staff, managers, and organizations. The qualities were drawn from our own experiences as members of our public library's Innovation Team and are meant to be not prescriptive or comprehensive but a starting point for developing your own approach to innovation.

Communication

Transparent communication, active listening, and positive storytelling can help individuals and organizations to create a foundation for innovation. Open channels of communication allow for and encourage the free exchange and collaborative development of ideas. Effective communication reinforces that ideas are valued and builds understanding of organizational history and current efforts.

Transparency

Communication from the beginner's mind is open and honest. This type of communication does not hide from hard truths or from emotional responses but expresses them freely and respectfully. For managers, being transparent means being able to communicate clearly to staff about why and how decisions are made in your organization. Modeling for staff how to communicate truthfully and respectfully creates an environment where employees feel safe to do the same. As Suzuki (1997) noted, "You should be true to your feelings, and to your mind, expressing yourself without any reservations. This helps the listener to understand more easily" (87).

At the organizational level, transparency means providing all staff with access to documentation of the decision-making process, including leadership meeting minutes, updates about ongoing work group projects, and progress on goals. This information should be easily accessible to any staff. Also, providing the history behind past decisions and ideas about future decisions allows all staff to know where the organization has been and enables staff to develop informed perspectives about possible new directions.

Listening

One of the most critical and immediate things you can do is to listen to your colleagues, your supervisors, and those you supervise. Try to approach listening without eagerness to share your own opinions. Focus instead on what you hear. Don't try to form arguments to support your position, but rather take in the perspectives of others.

Try this in your next meeting: Listen carefully, ask questions to clarify, and don't make assumptions. If you aren't sure, ask. Your colleagues' ideas and solutions may not be obvious or fully formed even once spoken. Rather than trying to "win" or make your opinion triumph over others, just listen. "Try not to force your ideas on someone, but rather think about it with him. If you feel you have won the discussion, that also is the wrong attitude. Try not to win in the argument; just listen to it; but it is also wrong to behave as if you had lost" (Suzuki 1997, 91).

This kind of openness in listening can happen anywhere in your organization. As part of an organizational culture, openness in listening can encourage respect for a variety of perspectives, forge new understandings about the many roles and responsibilities within your organization, and create connections. In the words of Suzuki: "When you listen to someone, you should give up all your preconceived ideas and your subjective opinions; you should just listen to him, just observe what his way is. We put very little emphasis on right and wrong or good and bad. We just see things as they are with him, and accept them" (Suzuki 1997, 87).

Storytelling

Managers must share a common language and common definitions about what it means to innovate. Telling the story of what it means to innovate in your own organization helps build this common language that everyone can use: "Through your master's language, you understand more than what his words actually say" (Suzuki 1997, 86–87). Having a way to communicate the story of your organization and how your mission and goals add value in the communities you serve will help to create a shared vision at all levels. By telling these stories, the whole organization can build upon this shared knowledge and vision and be inspired to continue to find new ways to be successful in achieving the goals of your organization.

Tell the stories of innovations large and small by staff everywhere in your organization. Managers and staff alike can share stories of how they or their colleagues have successfully brought to the table and executed their ideas, always making the connection to how these successes furthered organizational goals. Staff will see that they add value to the services you provide by bringing forward their ideas.

Perception

How we view the world can greatly affect our ability to innovate. Diverse perspectives ensure that more ideas are explored and refined. Nonattachment helps us to try out new ideas even if we may fail, to freely share and collaborate, and to move on when necessary. Having a powerful vision for your organization ensures that innovations move your organization in the direction you want.

Diverse Perspectives

You are just one person and cannot see all of the possibilities on your own. Know that you don't know everything. Seek out the perspectives of others both within and outside of your organization. Cultivating a beginner's mind helps you remember that you don't know, and can't know, every best solution or best new service. As Suzuki (1997) noted, "In the beginner's mind there are many possibilities, but in the expert's there are few" (21).

The literature of innovation offers many suggestions for utilizing diverse perspectives in the service of innovation. Bason (2010) argues that it takes courage to relinquish control but that managers must do this in order to embrace the divergence of ideas and perspectives that feed innovation (29). Tom Kelley (2005), of design and innovation consulting firm IDEO, suggests encouraging diversity in several ways. First, "give your team greater variety and they will start seeing the outlines of new connections, making new leaps of imagination" (79). Next, hire for diversity. Don't hire someone just because he or she is like one of your best employees (72). Finally, enlist informal mentors to gain new and fresh perspectives: "Sometimes what managers really need is a mentor from a younger generation to inform and inspire" (86).

As an organization, the library is many things to many people. Libraries serve a variety of needs and provide diverse experiences and services to all members of our communities. "The library" means something different to all of the people we serve. We can seek out the perspectives of our community about what the library means to different types of users and use this diversity of perspectives to create and strengthen services in our community.

Internally, our organizations rely on a diversity of skills and knowledge to run smoothly: facilities and maintenance workers keep our spaces functional and clean; librarians conduct reference interviews to get at the information needs of customers; circulation staff understand the variety of issues with patron accounts and skillfully move users through policies and procedures; managers support and coach staff and build teams. The individual in each of these roles holds a particular perspective about the library, its purpose in the community, and how he or she fits into the larger organization. Utilizing the diversity of perspectives within our organizations allows us to understand how we all work together and helps us to provide better service to our users. Create opportunities for staff from a variety of departments and designations to get together and make connections. Avoid being what Bason (2010) called a "mono-professional culture" that doesn't allow for "constructive clashes" across disciplines which are "often a catalyst for radical new solutions" (16–17).

Nonattachment

Bason (2010) pointed out that strong professional identities lead to the inability to try and fail (17). We imagine that our continued success relies on maintaining an identity that we have worked very hard at achieving. However, this attitude holds us back from trying new things. In Suzuki's (1997) words: "In the beginner's mind there is no thought, 'I have attained something.' All self-centered thoughts limit our vast mind. When we have no thought of achievement, no thought of self, we are true beginners. Then we can really learn something" (22).

When we bring our ideas to bear and create new services, we do it in the spirit of serving our communities. Creating in the spirit of service is similar to the Zen Buddhist concept of *dana prajna paramita*, which literally means: to give (*dana*), wisdom (*prajna*), to cross over or reach the other shore (*paramita*) (Suzuki 1997, 66). We give our skills and knowledge over to the community to create services and resources that add value. We can do this as members of a team, giving our good ideas to the group to forward our mission. We can work together in the spirit of service and not cling to our ideas but give them away.

Don't be attached to your good ideas or to the problems around you. It is easy to get caught up in the latest disagreeable policy change or cultural constraint affecting your organization. Don't allow yourself to be attached to these issues; look at these problems simply as part of everything. This can free us up to see opportunities and release us from struggles that sap our energy and distract us from our mission. As Suzuki (1997) noted, "Only because you seek to gain something through rigid formal practice does it become a problem for you. But if we appreciate whatever problem we have as an expression of big mind [accepting everything as it is, everything is everything], it is not a problem anymore" (92).

Powerful Vision

Having a beginner's mind means keeping the big picture in mind. Organizations with a clearly defined vision provide a framework for all staff to contribute to the larger goals of the organization. Suzuki (1997) wrote, "And we should do something new. To do something new, of course we must know our past.... But we should not keep holding onto anything we have done; we should only reflect on it. And we must have some idea of what we should do in the future" (71). Writing for the *Innovation Excellence* blog, Jeffrey Phillips (2010) asserted, "Without a vision to strive towards, the [innovation] team can't make headway. A good vision should stretch the organization and take them out of their comfort zone, since you really can't innovate while resting comfortably in your little cocoon."

If your organization has not yet articulated a clear vision and mission, you can work with your colleagues and your supervisor to articulate the goals of your own unit within the larger organization. Don't wait for leadership to articulate these for you. Collaborate with your colleagues and find your vision. Continue discussing this vision and connecting it to the work you do every day. By articulating a vision, you can bring focus and relevance to the creation of new ideas, resulting in greater value for your community.

Action

Innovation ultimately requires action. When we think about innovation, we often think about big changes that affect many people. However, small-scale actions that we take on our own, including shifting our mind-sets or adjusting our attitudes, can be equally important. Collaborating, maintaining calm and patience, and accepting realities and challenges along the way are actions you can take now to enable successful innovation in your organization.

Collaboration

We have discussed how bringing a diverse group of people to the table brings more perspectives and ideas to drive innovation. Frontline staff can collaborate informally by talking with one another about the ideas they have, asking questions of staff in other departments and designations and drawing on their expertise in order to create something together. It may seem intimidating or even inappropriate to approach a manager or a colleague in another part of your organization, but most people will be glad that you asked for their input and will enjoy talking about the work that they do. Opportunities to collaborate also improve employee satisfaction by tapping into people's innate creativity: "Moment after moment we are creating something, and this is the joy of our life" (Suzuki 1997, 65).

Managers can provide opportunities for collaborations across designations, creating richer results and innovative service. An example of this is from a library where a manager facilitated an opportunity for a librarian and a circulation desk worker to go together to the local farmer's market. Although there was pushback for allowing circulation staff to participate in outreach, traditionally done only by librarians, this manager made the case for circulation staff to be on hand to provide information about library cards and accounts. This resulted in successful outreach and demonstrated the value of collaboration across designations in providing service.

Collaborate with your community as well. Bason (2010) argued that processes of co-creation, building on the principle of citizen involvement, are a key dimension in the ecosystem of public sector innovation (27). One example of community collaboration is from a readers' advisory service that provided book suggestions from librarians on Facebook. The library's Facebook followers chimed in with their own reading suggestions for their fellow community members. Our communities are ready to collaborate if we give them the chance.

Patience and Calm

Changing the culture of a large organization can be excruciatingly slow. Keep in mind that change happens gradually and sometimes slower than we would like. Having patience with the process will be extremely helpful when hashing out new ideas with your team, experimenting and sometimes failing. Suzuki (1997) wrote, "Even though you try very hard, the progress you make is always little by little. It is not like going out in a shower in which you know when you get wet. In a fog, you do not know you are getting wet, but as you keep walking you get wet little by little" (46).

Once things begin to start moving, maintain this patient attitude. Try not to get swept up and carried off by the wave of change. Stay grounded in your vision. Stay calm. "But if we become interested in some excitement, or in our own change, we will become completely involved in our busy life, and we will be lost. But if your mind is calm and constant, you can keep yourself away from the noisy world even though you are in the midst of it. In the midst of noise and change, your mind will be quiet and stable" (Suzuki 1997, 57–58).

Openness and Acceptance

Accepting the realities of your organization, the current organizational structure, the constraints of less than adequate budgets, the current capacity of staff to innovate, and the slow rate of progress, one can begin to think realistically about what can be done within this context. The beginner's mind is open to things as they are. Having this mind-set allows you to look at the realities in front of you with clarity, with a descriptive rather than prescriptive perspective. In Suzuki's (1997) words: "A mind full of preconceived ideas, subjective intentions, or habits is not open to things as they are" (88).

Tom Kelley (2005), in discussing innovation efforts in private sector organizations, recognized that "innovation teams often hurdle barriers set up by well-meaning management" (99). Barriers to innovation come from everywhere. Being open and accepting can help you, not only to see things as they are and work within that reality, but also to embrace criticism and turn it into a positive force. Kelley encouraged companies trying to innovate to "embrace your critics" (139). Do not ignore or explain away complaints from your staff or users. Consider and accept criticism and use it to your favor.

Conclusion

Given the shifting landscape of technology and the diminishing boundaries across cultures and societies, it has never been more important for libraries to be responsive and flexible in order to fulfill their missions. Libraries must become innovative organizations that both provide innovative services to a diverse community of users and help to ensure that communities have the tools they need to come together and innovate. By adopting qualities of a beginner's mind, individuals and organizations can begin to create the organizational culture necessary to fulfill their vital role in society.

SUGGESTED READINGS

Bason, Christian. *Leading Public Sector Innovation: Co-creating for a Better Society.* Bristol, UK: Policy Press, 2010.

Kelley, Tom. *The Ten Faces of Innovation: IDEO's Strategies for Beating the Devil's Advocate and Driving Creativity throughout Your Organization.* New York: Doubleday, 2005.

Suzuki, Shunryu. *Zen Mind, Beginner's Mind: Informal Talks on Zen Meditation and Practice.* 13th ed. Edited by Trudy Dixon. New York: Weatherhill, 1997.

REFERENCES

Bason, Christian. 2010. *Leading Public Sector Innovation: Co-creating for a Better Society.* Bristol, UK: Policy Press.

Berger, Warren. 2012. "What Zen Taught Silicon Valley (and Steve Jobs) about Innovation." *Co.DESIGN* (blog), April 9. www.fastcodesign.com/1669387/what-zen-taught-silicon-valley-and-steve-jobs-about-innovation.

Godin, Seth. 2008. *Tribes: We Need You to Lead Us.* New York: Penguin Group.

Google Inc. 2013. "Ten Things We Know to Be True." About Google—What We Believe. Accessed March 15. www.google.com/about/company/philosophy.

Kelley, Tom. 2005. *The Ten Faces of Innovation: IDEO's Strategies for Beating the Devil's Advocate and Driving Creativity throughout Your Organization.* New York: Doubleday.

Phillips, Jeffrey. 2010. "Vision and Passion for Innovation Success." *Innovation Excellence* (blog), June 10. www.innovationexcellence.com/blog/2010/06/10/vision-and-passion-for-innovation-success.

SICP (Office of Social Innovation and Civic Participation). 2013. "About SICP—The Community Solutions Agenda." The White House Official Homepage. Accessed March 15. www.whitehouse.gov/administration/eop/sicp/about.

Suzuki, Shunryu. 1997. *Zen Mind, Beginner's Mind: Informal Talks on Zen Meditation and Practice.* 13th ed. Edited by Trudy Dixon. New York: Weatherhill.

2

. . . . . .

Driving Creativity and
Innovation in Your Organization

It's Easier Than You Think

Kelly Pepo

D
o you ever come across an idea beyond the library realm and think, "Hey, I could see that working in my library!" Or do you keep bumping into that new, hot thing, like quick response (QR) codes, vending machines, or 3-D printers and wonder how your library can capitalize on the momentum? Incorporating a committee, team, or even a single point person in an organization to actively monitor trends and seek inspiration beyond the profession is essential in a time when it seems that change itself is changing faster than organizations can keep up. How do libraries stay connected to our patrons and their ever-growing interests and the technology that seems to be evolving more and more quickly?

In 2005, a representative from the Orange County Library System (OCLS) in Florida attended a one-day seminar presented by Trendwatching.com. The most important takeaway from the day was this: *Every* organization, big or small, should have some kind of structured plan or process to track local and global trends. It is easy to become overwhelmed at the thought of attempting to harness these trends and realities and to let these moments of inspiration pass you by. But wait! Don't give up! Believe it or not, tracking trends and identifying how they can connect your services to your patrons and even enhance the programs, products, and experiences you already offer can be *fun*. Yes, that's right—*fun!* OCLS has created its very own team of trend-watching idea developers to shepherd ideas from mere inspiration to implementation. They are the Innovation Champions (ICs).

Before the ICs were formed, trend watching and idea development lacked the structure and focus of a dedicated and formal committee. In 2005, following the Trendwatching.com seminar, OCLS formed the Trendwatchers Committee. Composed of volunteers from various positions and departments throughout the system, the committee's official mission was to disseminate information about global trends and *translate ideas into viable projects and services*, a mission that still holds true today for the ICs. The group met monthly either face-to-face or online to discuss which trends they had observed and potential ideas for the library to explore. The committee elected to use an internal wiki and later a public blog to monitor trends, to track articles and concepts shared outside of the committee, and to create a page of resources to capture what websites, blogs, periodicals, RSS feeds, and so forth, were "out there" to track trends.

While the Trendwatchers Committee was monitoring and sharing trends, another committee was formed. The Orange Seed also consisted of staff from various positions and departments throughout the system. The purpose was to encourage employees to submit ideas to a blog (utilized by staff but open to the public for viewing and comment) using an online form to define the concept of their ideas. These ideas were evaluated by the committee and the administrative team for viability and then posted for the organization at large to review and vote on for implementation. If an idea was selected, the staff member was rewarded with additional hours of vacation time.

In the meantime, another group called the Innovation Team was formed. This was a team of staff selected to meet regularly with the library director to discuss what new innovations were taking off and how they might apply to libraries. These employees were identified for inclusion based on being tech savvy and having an interest in innovation. For meetings, the director often provided articles or topics of discussion or ran it as an open forum during which the group would drive conversation. It was apparent that a theme was evolving with these separate committees all striving to harness the ideas and creativity of the entire organization. There is power in numbers instead of relying on the input of a few to drive the development of an organization and its goals.

In 2010, the administrative team evaluated this structure and determined that the library had three different groups trying to accomplish the same, relative objective. The groups were combined into one new committee called the Innovation Champions to continue driving OCLS forward in its efforts to stay abreast of emerging trends and technologies. Members of the committee would continue to monitor trends and contribute ideas. They would also support staff with ideas and foster idea development throughout the organization. Ideally, staff would not only be empowered to suggest ideas and share trends, but they would also take an active role in the evaluation, development, and execution of proposed ideas.

Once the concept of the ICs was in place, staff from various positions and departments, including librarians, managers, technology trainers, and clerks, were selected to be a part of the team. When searching for potential candidates, the administration sought out exceptional and enthusiastic employees with the potential to "think outside of the library box." The chairs from both the Trendwatchers Committee and the Orange Seed came together to co-chair this new group.

At the inception of the new committee, the group met to crystallize its mission and to establish expectations. Discovering trends and generating ideas had turned out not to be much of a problem, but putting the ideas into action was another story. This committee was charged with creating a procedure by which the kernel of an idea is carried through the idea development process. They also needed to identify how they, as a group, could support the organization and individuals with idea development.

One of the first steps was to identify what the evolution of an idea actually looked like from start to finish. Identifying a potential idea, the committee used it to physically diagram the journey of an idea to illustrate the different roads and detours an idea could take before arriving at its final destination. Glogster.com, a real idea by an ICs committee member, was ideal to diagram as a potential idea. Ultimately, implementation of the idea was not feasible at the time, but this only further served to reinforce that when an idea is determined impractical for OCLS, it can still serve as a learning process. While not every idea comes to fruition, sometimes the idea spins off into another version with greater potential (see figure 2.1). In this instance, the purpose of this idea was to illustrate the idea process to the organization

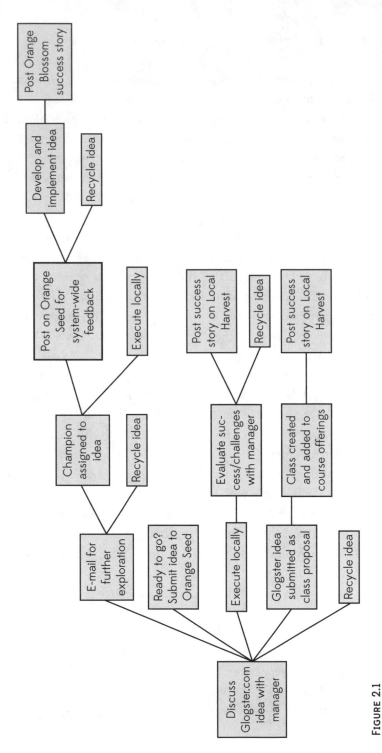

Figure 2.1
Journey of an Idea

and to serve as a springboard for talking points as the committee introduced how to evaluate ideas to all staff at OCLS.

It was also necessary to identify a tool the ICs could use to communicate trends, articles, and ideas as well as to establish a place for all staff to go to submit an idea. One of the former committees, the Orange Seed, had already created a blog to submit and track ideas as well as to acknowledge ideas put into action. With a little modification, the blog was renovated to serve as a similar tool for the ICs. One of the key components of this resource was an idea submission form. Structured to capture the concept of the idea, the form also required the submitter to explore the idea's actual viability in some detail and depth through these questions:

1. What are the details of your idea?
2. Which part of the library's strategic plan does this idea support and how?
3. What are the costs versus benefits of your idea?
4. What role will you play in the implementation?

The intent of this form is for the initiator to be an active participant in executing the idea. It is not uncommon for a person to have a great idea and then hand it over to someone else. If the idea is outside of a person's expertise, he or she is at least encouraged to think about his or her role in supporting the idea, whether this would be acting as its ambassador or in another smaller role. Regarding cost, not all staff members are accustomed to looking at an idea or process in terms of dollars. The cost-versus-benefits question requires the idea initiator to itemize details such as labor, printing, supplies, equipment, and so on. Requesting staff to consider where an idea falls within the objectives of the strategic plan and the library's resources ensures that everyone in the organization is working to support the library's overarching goals.

In addition to the idea form, the blog features five Orange Seed categories: Germinate, Local Harvest, Orange Blossoms, Put on the Shelf, and Seedlings (see figure 2.2):

- *Germinate:* Once an idea has been submitted and its viability reviewed by library administration, it is placed on the Germinate page. Here, all staff members are able to see the idea

FIGURE 2.2
Orange Seed Categories

and offer support, suggestions, or constructive criticism as to whether the idea should continue to move forward. An idea does not have to receive feedback or comments to move forward, but placing an idea here provides the opportunity for staff to identify further potential or possible pitfalls in the success of the idea. Ultimately, library administration makes the final decision to continue going forward with an idea, particularly if there is significant cost or investment of resources involved.

- *Local Harvest:* Many people believe that an idea must be an earth-shattering thought that will completely transform an organization and leave a large footprint. But ideas come in all shapes and sizes and from all corners of an organization. Local Harvest is the place to showcase ideas already in action. Staff from different locations can share what they are doing that may be of value to other departments or inspire further creativity and solutions. Whether it is recycling unused book covers to make colorful displays or putting hairspray on a whiteboard to keep little hands from smudging promotions, the projects featured on Local Harvest highlight the successes of different departments and spread the word so that others can implement the ideas, too.

- *Orange Blossoms:* Once an idea has been approved and put into action, it becomes an official Orange Blossom. This page is a snapshot of developed ideas that staff can visit to evaluate the overall success of the ideas.

- *Put on the Shelf:* Not every idea makes it to Germinate or Orange Blossoms, but the idea may be the seed of a concept that will be worth revisiting later on. Sometimes the necessary technology is not yet available, or the resources to fully invest in the idea are lacking. Putting ideas "on the shelf" prevents them from becoming lost as new ideas keep emerging.

- *Seedlings:* As Innovation Champions follow and monitor various idea trackers, they will discover many different types of activities, products, or services that may have relevance or provide inspiration to OCLS. These "seedlings" of ideas are captured and posted so that everyone in the organization can read and comment on the possibilities of whether they can spin off into something new and exciting for library patrons. Content is not exclusive to the ICs, with some articles being contributed by staff outside of the committee. Examples include sharing a recently discovered article or website, a photo of a display or event attended while at a conference, or an out-of-work activity that inspires an idea for discussion and exploration.

Once the committee finalized these tools and established the direction of its charge, the next step was to introduce the organization to the Innovation Champions and the Orange Seed blog. Every quarter, the library director visits each branch in the system, bringing along a featured guest speaker from a different department, an ideal opportunity for the ICs to reach as many staff as possible face-to-face. The ICs asked to be the next featured guest to launch its "campaign." Representatives from the ICs team accompanied the director on visits to all fifteen locations. They shared a crafted presentation to familiarize staff with the role of the committee, what the journey of an idea looked like, and how to seek the support of an IC if they had an idea they needed help developing. The committee also conducted a brief brainstorming session to encourage participants to share ideas, which were later reviewed and then followed up on to discuss the ideas and their feasibility.

The staff intranet functions as an ongoing reminder of the committee and what is happening, featuring regular posts of information and shared ideas and offering employees a venue to post comments and contribute new ideas. It also includes a link to the Orange Seed blog for easy access. Committee members are expected to motivate colleagues to engage in the process.

Part of being an engaged Innovation Champion is actively seeking and monitoring resources to identify trends and how they can inspire new library products, services, and other concepts. There are many different resources available. Where does one look for inspiration? Try some of these websites to get started:

- Trendwatching.com
- Mashable.com
- Springwise.com
- Influxinsights.com
- TED.com
- Trendhunter.com
- PSFK.com

Or sometimes inspiration is closer to home:

- Newspapers, white papers, websites, magazines, blogs
- Television, movies, radio
- Customers, co-workers, friends, family
- Competitors
- Shops, museums, hotels, airports
- Eavesdropping, chat rooms, day-to-day conversations

There is no bad place to look for new ideas, inspiration, or innovation. What may not strike a chord in one person could provide a wealth of ideas for another. Check out a few sources and see where they lead. If they do not meet your expectations or fail to motivate you, move on to something new.

What are key components for an organization to implement its own trend-watching plan? First, there needs to be administrative buy-in. The leaders of the organization must recognize and *support* (big difference) the need for an individual or a group to be actively engaged in staying abreast of what is going on outside of the library's physical and virtual walls. This means support for the investment of staff time to monitor and research trends plus an understanding that some ideas may require an investment of funds.

Maybe each idea is handled on a case-by-case basis, or perhaps there is a budget set aside for idea development. Individual budgets will dictate the dollar limit on what can be tried at any given time. What is more critical is having an environment that supports the freedom of ideas and the freedom to fail. It is not realistic to expect every idea to be successful, and all parties involved need to be okay with that in order to keep a positive attitude about sharing new ideas.

In addition, there needs to be staff buy-in. There is power in numbers, and the more people involved, the greater the opportunity for success. What is difficult to convey is that anyone can be a trend watcher or innovator. There is no special skill or training required, only a willingness to try looking at what is going on to see if there is a way to harness those interests to identify new products or services. It could even mean reinventing how to introduce existing products and services already connected to those trends. What staff do not always remember is that they are not only library employees but also consumers, library users, and often a snapshot of what makes up their library's community. If there is an idea that speaks to them, it could appeal to others as well.

Buy-in is the greatest challenge in establishing this type of initiative. While the Orange Seed blog has been utilized by some staff and reminders on the intranet invite short bursts of interest, it has not sustained the desired interest and buy-in as hoped. Buy-in has certainly been the biggest hurdle for OCLS, and there are a few different reasons why this could be. It is difficult for staff to look at trend watching as part of their jobs. They often see it as a task that falls low on their to-do list. Dedicating time to thinking of new ideas when they are busy implementing others and maintaining excellent customer service can be perceived as just one more thing to do. Also, they may not be sure where to submit their ideas nor be willing to invest the time it takes to do so; with the blog, they can do this easily and relatively quickly.

There is also the intimidation factor of taking an idea forward. Depending on what their positions are, staff may be unable to see an idea beyond what it is, much less figure out the specifics of making it a reality. Reaching out to their manager or an Innovation Champion may not be within their comfort zone. To nurture the buy-in atmosphere, it could be helpful to hold brainstorming sessions on a particular topic at staff meetings, share an article directly with the group to solicit their thoughts, or consider inviting an Innovation Champion to give a presentation. Staff are always encouraged (and somewhat required) to consult with their manager as a first level of discussion, and the manager has the opportunity to support staff by directing them to the ICs to support them both.

From an administrative perspective, libraries have had a turbulent few years with budgets and staffing. The importance of incorporating an initiative that may require additional resources could prove to be a tricky argument to make. What is critical to convey is that it is in the best interests of the organization to recognize that moving forward requires a connection to what is happening in today's society. As libraries strive to remain relevant to current users and at the same time appeal to new ones, it is beneficial to invest both the time and the money tracking what is keeping patrons' attention.

The Innovation Champions effort remains a work in progress for OCLS. The organization continues to explore how to best engage employees for contributions and feedback and to identify what is the appropriate method to track trends and apply what is gleaned toward future planning. Some notable successes include a customized welcome e-mail to new card holders, a library card intervention (www.ocls.info/intervention), using QR codes for online library card registration, and using EggBot technology for maker programs and classes (www.ocls.info/Virtual/Videos/Innovations/eggbot.asp). No matter which direction this process takes, there are some dos and don'ts learned along the way.

Do:

- *Create a space to track trends and ideas.* It is a good practice to maintain a record of proposed ideas and successes that provides quantifiable benchmarks.

- *Try stuff out!* Talking and getting excited about ideas is only part of seeing what will work. Hands-on action is the best way to tell if there is potential.

- *Monitor trends regularly.* What's popular changes constantly, and the only way to stay connected is to review sources consistently. Schedule a reminder or subscribe to a few sources to establish ongoing engagement.

- *Look cross-industry.* Find inspiration for libraries outside of the profession. Be open-minded when exploring what other industries are doing and what works for them.

Don't:

- *Be overwhelmed.* Yes, there is a tremendous amount of information available to track trends. Celebrate that there is too much and not too little.

- *Be short-sighted.* Try not to dismiss trends or what others are doing because it has already been done. Just because it is not new to libraries does not mean it is not worth pursuing at your library. Be okay with not being the first if it adds value to your patrons' experience.

- *Dismiss fads.* Although fads can be fleeting, they still indicate popularity and interest among patrons. A program, display, or other products based on a fad could be the key factor for bringing in a new user group, offering the opportunity to hook them on all of the other great library services available.

See also Trendwatching.com for "15 Trend Tips" that offer helpful guidelines and a place to get started (http://trendwatching.com/trends/pdf/trendwatching%202010-10%20Tips.pdf).

The Innovation Champions committee and its processes for trend watching and idea development will continue to evolve. As its history has shown, it is important to review committee efforts, what is and is not working, and what can be improved. Moving forward, OCLS will continue to actively track trends and to seek new and innovative ways to convert those trends into products and services for its patrons. Take a moment to identify how your library can implement its own method for reaching out into the vastness of what is going on with universal trends and technologies. The possibilities are unlimited as to what this could generate.

3

The Library's Role in Promoting Tolerance and Diversity in a University

Lorna E. Rourke

The emphasis on the Roman Catholic tradition was something I noted when I applied for the position of librarian at St. Jerome's University (SJU) in 2007, but the stated adherence to the principles of academic freedom was a reassuring complement to the religious tradition. At my job interview, I asked how working at a Roman Catholic institution would affect my role as librarian. I stated that I could not work in a university in which my ability to choose materials for the library, conduct information literacy sessions, and plan activities would be compromised by the necessity to adhere to religious principles. In conversations with faculty and administrators at the university, I was assured that there would not be restrictions on my academic freedom at SJU. In fact, I was told of the diversity of the community, in which people teach, work, and study regardless of religious affiliation or sexual orientation. I heard about academic programs like Sexuality, Marriage, and the Family (SMF), in which courses such as "The Dark Side of Sexuality" and "Sexual Ethics" are taught from a liberal viewpoint. I accepted the position and began my career as the only librarian at SJU.

In general, I have found SJU to be an open-minded environment in which I am able to manage the library guided by principles of intellectual freedom. Occasionally I have been asked to remove books from the library, including books seen as too orthodox as well as those seen as heterodox, and have kept them all on the shelves. Activities in the library and throughout SJU encompass a vast range of subjects, speakers, and opinions. Different viewpoints are represented in classes, meetings, and events.

At the University of Waterloo (UW), a series of lectures called the Pascal Lectures on Christianity and the University has taken place every year since 1978. These lectures have featured such internationally renowned thinkers as Malcolm Muggeridge, Madeleine L'Engle, and Margaret Visser and are intended to feature "outstanding individuals of international repute who have distinguished themselves in both an area of scholarly endeavor and an area of Christian thought or life" (University of Waterloo 2013). In early 2012, we learned that that year's lecture would be given by Charles Rice, a professor emeritus at the University of Notre Dame Law School. A faculty member involved in planning Dr. Rice's visit contacted me. She informed me that, in addition to the Pascal lecture, Dr. Rice would be speaking to some classes and presenting a seminar at SJU. She asked me to purchase all of his books for the library, some in multiple copies. When I reviewed the titles being requested, I could see that they were written from an ultraconservative viewpoint, one that I do not share. However, as librarian, I am responsible for ensuring that our collection presents a variety of opinions, so I used part of this professor's acquisitions budget allocation to buy several of Dr. Rice's books, including *The Winning Side: Questions on Living the Culture of Life* and *What Happened to Notre Dame?*

It was not until weeks later that I became aware of the controversy surrounding Dr. Rice's visit to the UW campus. E-mails began circulating among UW and SJU faculty regarding Dr. Rice's views. For example, he is a proponent of the traditional teachings of the *Catechism of the Catholic Church* (Liberia Editrice Vaticana 2003), particularly sections such as 2357:

> Homosexuality refers to relations between men or between women who experience an exclusive or predominant sexual attraction toward persons of the same sex.... tradition has always declared that "homosexual acts are intrinsically disordered." They are contrary to the natural law. They close the sexual act to the gift of life.... Under no circumstances can they be approved.

Dr. Rice (2010) moved beyond these teachings of the Catholic Church in his view that homosexual unions may lead to polygamy and bestiality:

> [I]f individual choice prevails without regard to limits of nature, how can the choice be limited to two persons? Polygamy (one man, multiple women), polyandry (one woman, multiple men), polyamory (sexual relations between or among multiple persons of one or both sexes) and other possible arrangements, involving the animal kingdom as well, would derive legitimacy from the same contraceptive premise that justifies one-on-one homosexual relations.

When people learned of his views, some questioned this choice of speaker for a prestigious lecture on the campus of a nonreligious, publicly funded university. Even at SJU, a Roman Catholic university, some faculty, staff, and students found the choice of Dr. Rice as Pascal lecturer an unfortunate one. I was among those concerned about the choice. Some faculty asked to have the invitation to Dr. Rice rescinded and a more appropriate, less controversial speaker invited; these requests were not acted upon. At least one member of the Pascal Committee resigned over the selection of Dr. Rice.

Academic freedom and intellectual freedom are among the most important values of a university and a library. While I was not supportive of the choice of Dr. Rice as Pascal lecturer, I recognize the right of anyone to express his or her opinion, especially in a university, as upheld in the Canadian Charter of Rights and Freedoms and other statements. However, it was clear to me and to some colleagues that the presence of Dr. Rice on campus and the apparent support for his visit and his teachings could be hurtful to some members of the university, particularly the LGBTQ (lesbian, gay, bisexual, transgender, queer) community. Some perceived that Dr. Rice's views had wide support on campus because he was giving a prestigious lecture introduced by the president of SJU and he was being given the opportunity to speak directly to students in some classes and to faculty during a seminar. It was essential to seek opportunities for alternative points of view to be presented on campus during the same time period that Dr. Rice's opinions were being aired. I partnered with two SJU faculty members, Dr. Steven Bednarski from Medieval Studies and Dr. Tracy Penny Light from SMF, to plan events and activities to counterbalance the others. Informally, we called ourselves the Ad Hoc Tolerance Committee.

The activities we planned and participated in took place at the large university next to ours, at our own small university, and in the library. Newspaper articles, letters to the editor, and interviews were published in local and campus newspapers, informing the community about the controversy surrounding Dr. Rice's visit and his appointment as Pascal lecturer. At the University of Waterloo, Philosophy professor Dr. Shannon Dea organized a "Rainbow celebration"—a silent, peaceful protest that took place just outside the hall in which Dr. Rice's Pascal lecture was to occur. This protest was intended as a show of solidarity for the LGBTQ community at UW, in light of the lecture being given by someone who "sees homosexuality as a 'moral disorder' and is opposed to gay marriage" (Mercer 2012). As Philosophy professor Dr. Tim Kenyon noted, "all the messages I have seen about the silent protest have been extremely clear and consistent about the importance of respecting the freedom of speech. The silent protest is focused on the decision to honour Dr. Rice, and not on his freedom to utter whatever sentences may strike him as worth uttering" (Panchoo 2012).

As an untenured member of the academic staff, I had some concerns about being seen as a participant in the protest, particularly because the president of SJU would be introducing Dr. Rice at the lecture and because I knew that my supervisor, the dean, would be attending. However, I felt it was most important to show my support for LGBTQ colleagues and students, so I joined 100 others outside the Modern Languages building as the eighty people who attended the lecture filed past. It was indeed a peaceful protest. As the newspaper reported the following day, "the university beefed up security inside and outside the theatre on Tuesday, with at least four paid-duty Waterloo Regional Police officers on hand to bolster the ranks of several campus police officers. No incidents were reported and no one disrupted the talk" (Davis 2012).

At SJU, Dr. Rice's lectures and seminars, presented to Philosophy classes and to selected members of the faculty and administration, proceeded as planned, undisturbed by anyone. In the library, I mounted a book display that featured materials on tolerance and inclusivity as a counterbalance to what I knew students were hearing in some of their classes that week. Titles in the display included John Boswell's *Christianity, Social Tolerance,* and Homosexuality: Gay People in Western Europe from the Beginning of the Christian Era to the Fourteenth Century; Louis Crompton's Homosexuality and Civilization; Martin Kantor's Homophobia: The State of Sexual Bigotry Today; and Rachel and Sarah Hagger-Holt's Living It Out: A Survival Guide for Lesbian, Gay and Bisexual Christians and Their Friends, Families and Churches. The display also featured a poster promoting the Rainbow protest and other tolerance-related events that were happening at that time. I took the opportunity to purchase additional books, reflecting both sides of the issue, to ensure that our collection represented a diversity of opinions. I promoted the week's events on our Facebook page and the university's website. I capitalized on a large, free-standing display board inside the front doors of the library to highlight the themes of tolerance and inclusivity, covering the board with posters promoting the week's events and images from homopositive book covers. I included quotations ranging from Bara Dada's "Jesus is ideal and wonderful, but you Christians—you are not like him" (Jones 1925, 114), to Jimmy Carter's "Jesus never said a word about homosexuality.... He never said that gay people should be condemned" (Raushenbush 2012), to Melissa Etheridge's (1993) "Mothers, tell your children: be quick, you must be strong. Life is full of wonder, love is never wrong," and others.

Our Ad Hoc Tolerance Committee organized "An Evening of Christian Tolerance and Inclusivity," the culminating event of the week. While some members of our community opposed this activity and the other alternative events, we approached a number of different people and groups at SJU and ultimately gained the sponsorship and support of the Office of the Vice-President and Academic Dean and the department of Religious Studies in addition to the original sponsors—the Medieval Studies program, the library, and the SMF department. We were pleased that an idea which initially started with a few people had grown to include many others in the university. We promoted the event widely and sent invitations to members of our board of governors, the president of the university, reporters, and student and faculty groups. We chose a rainbow theme to illustrate our support for the LGBTQ community and to represent inclusiveness and diversity. Multicolored balloons decorated the stage; vases of colorful flowers were placed around the room; and we presented an array of rainbow-themed food, including multicolored popcorn and candy, brightly colored vegetables and fruit, rainbow chip cookies, and different colors of juice. All of this reinforced our theme while pleasing the eye and the taste buds. While the décor and refreshments were light-hearted, there was a serious tone to the evening, as the issues being addressed were so important.

The event, attended by over 100 faculty, staff, students, and community members, began with a talk by Dr. Jacqueline Murray, a medieval historian from the University of Guelph, titled "Christianity, Inclusivity, and Homosexuality: Views from the Middle Ages/Views from Medievalists." In his remarks following Dr. Murray's presentation, Dr. Bednarski noted that her talk "historicized, problematized, and contextualized Christian tolerance." Dr. Murray commented, "I am happy to speak about these issues as a historian of marriage, family and sexuality in the Catholic tradition, which I have studied all my adult life" (Pender 2012). Following Dr. Murray's talk, Dr. Penny Light introduced and screened *BeInclusive!*, a documentary film that investigates attitudes toward homosexuality on the UW campus. It was produced by students in the SMF program. Jenn Wunder, one of those students, noted, "The BeInclusive project seeks to promote a campus climate that is inclusive of marginalized and under- or misrepresented groups, in particular the LGBTQ community" (University of Waterloo 2010). It was especially important for us to include the student-produced film at this event so that the views of our student community could be acknowledged and heard.

While some of our colleagues did not agree with our decision to host the tolerance and inclusivity event, it was an overwhelming success. There were many comments afterward about how important and meaningful the evening had been. I was grateful to be copied in a follow-up e-mail to the dean and a group of faculty in which Dr. Bednarski noted that "Lorna...took a political risk and proved again why UW needs real academic librarians."

In reflecting upon these events and the greater implications of what took place, I realize that my participation demonstrated the three roles in which I find myself: as librarian, I was able to promote the values of tolerance and inclusivity through book and poster displays and by ensuring a balanced library collection; as an academic, I helped plan and execute an event that provided an intellectual and artistic voice for these values; and as a member of the SJU community, I participated in the "Rainbow celebration" protest event to show my support for LGBTQ students and colleagues.

I learned a great deal from the experiences of our week of tolerance and inclusivity. I was able to stand up for what I believed in, to ensure that all points of view were represented in the library collection and in our displays, to express my views in a respectful way, to listen to the opinions of others, and to utilize the tools at my disposal to make the library a place of thoughtful inquiry and debate. One of the values of librarianship of which I am most proud is our support for academic and intellectual freedom. The presence of Dr. Rice on campus provided an opportunity to listen to what his supporters were saying, to read extensively about both sides of the issue, to discuss the issue with colleagues, and to work with allies at the university. There is strength in numbers and in being part of a collective, and we were able to democratically express our opinions without belittling the opinions of others.

I urge other libraries and librarians to consider how they might demonstrate a value that is important to them, deal with a social justice issue, or react to a situation in their own campus or community in a positive way. Here is my advice:

- Ensure that you understand the situation and all sides of the issue.

- Consider what you can do in the library, through showcasing items from the collection, mounting displays, and using social media. It does not have to be complicated or expensive.

- Partner with others in your community—faculty, staff, students, and community members.

- Consider what resources you have at your disposal: Is there a local speaker you could invite or a film you could show? Are there student- or community-led initiatives you could highlight?

- Communicate respectfully at all times with proponents and opponents, and engage in respectful, open, knowledgeable dialogue. This is, of course, essential.

- Seek sponsors, for both financial and collegial reasons. The more groups and people willing to be seen as sponsors, the more credibility and resources your initiative will have. Once we had permission to include the Dean's Office as one of the sponsors for our event, people who felt uncertain about participating were more inclined to attend.

- Spread the word! Take advantage of Facebook, Twitter, e-mail, and websites. Contact reporters. Invite the president of the university, the mayor, the chief librarian, the chair of the board. They may not attend, but you are spreading awareness of your event and of an important cause.

- Follow up with thank-you notes to speakers, sponsors, and attendees. Be sure to maintain communication with those on the "other side" of the issue. You all have to work together afterward.

- Be diligent. Watch for the next opportunity to get involved.

Libraries have great power and great responsibility. Both of these can be used to promote values such as tolerance and inclusivity. It's not always easy. It's not always popular. But it is always right.

REFERENCES

Davis, Brent. 2012. "Peaceful Protest Greets Controversial Lecturer." *The Record*, March 20. www.therecord.com/news-story/2598993-peaceful-protest-greets-controversial-lecturer.

Etheridge, Melissa. 1993. "Silent Legacy." On *Yes I Am*, Island Records, compact disc.

Jones, Stanley E. 1925. *The Christ of the Indian Road*. New York: Abingdon Press.

Liberia Editrice Vaticana. 2003. "Chastity and Homosexuality." In *Catechism of the Catholic Church*. www.vatican.va/archive/ccc_css/archive/catechism/p3s2c2a6.htm.

Mercer, Greg. 2012. "Lecturer at UW Prompts Silent Vigil." *The Record*, March 20. www.therecord.com/news-story/2600144-lecturer-at-uw-prompts-silent-vigil-.

Panchoo, Calan. 2012. "Contentious Notre Dame Lecturer Greeted with Silent Protest by Waterloo Community." *Imprint*, March 25. www.uwimprint.ca/article/14-contentious-notre-dame-lecturer-greeted-with.

Pender, Terry. 2012. "Pair of Protests Will Accompany (Post Departure) Charles Rice Lecture." *The Record*, March 18. www.therecord.com/news-story/2598675-pair-of-protests-will-accompany-post-departure-charles-rice-lecture.

Raushenbush, Paul B. 2012. "President Jimmy Carter Authors New Bible Book, Answers Hard Biblical Questions." *The Huffington Post*, March 19. www.huffingtonpost.com/2012/03/19/president-jimmy-carter-bible-book_n_1349570.html.

Rice, Charles E. 2010. "Dr. Charles Rice: March 1 'Right or Wrong?' Column." *LifeSiteNews*, March 3. www.lifesitenews.com/news/archive//ldn/2010/mar/10030315.

University of Waterloo. 2010. "Book Launch Today, Film Showing Tomorrow." *University of Waterloo Daily Bulletin*, November 25. www.bulletin.uwaterloo.ca/2010/nov/25th.html.

———. 2013. "Mandate of the Pascal Lectures." The Pascal Lectures on Christianity and the University. Accessed October 19. www.adm.uwaterloo.ca/pascal/?mandate.

PART II

INNOVATIVE STAFF

4

· · · ─ ─ · ·

Innovation Wizardry

Sarah Strahl and Erica J. Christianson

L ibrary innovation may look like wizardry, but there's no real magic to it. What looks like magic to the outside observer is actually the resolve and open-mindedness to see beyond departmental boundaries and the day-to-day routine business of the library.

Divining the needs of your patrons before they know they have a need doesn't require a crystal ball, but it does involve using the evaluation tools at your disposal to gather information on trends and requests. While working at the Ela Area Public Library District in Lake Zurich, Illinois, we have realized that innovation requires the ability to get others to share a vision and commit to making that vision a reality. Successfully becoming an innovation "wizard" means growing, adapting, and looking at failures as opportunity. While this demystification process may seem frightening, the following lessons will help any wizard, or library employee, on his or her way.

Philosopher's Stone of Innovation

The most important lesson in innovation wizardry is the very first one: anyone can be an innovator. All it takes is dedication, determination, and cooperation. For innovation to grow, many voices and ideas need to be heard, and they can come from anywhere and anyone. Wizards are found in all walks of library life.

We have found that buy-in from and listening to all organizational voices is a crucial component for innovation; therefore, we realized that there was a need for an interdepartmental coalition of library technology trainers and power users. Membership is open to all staff and includes representatives from all departments. Since the group's inception four years ago, the goal of the Digital Materials Group has been to drive technology innovation in the library. To meet this goal, the group has developed unique and engaging technology training initiatives for staff and patrons, created an e-reader circulation program (and a revamp of the same program), and hosted a technology petting zoo.

Building cross-departmental initiatives, such as a Digital Materials Group, is extremely important in libraries because we tend to put ourselves in knowledge silos or divide ourselves departmentally to the detriment of progress for the whole organization. Digital materials and services are everyone's responsibility and don't belong to a particular desk or department. Children's librarians have as much to contribute as adult reference librarians or circulation staff members. So, in the Digital Materials Group, everyone has a seat at the decision-making table and an active role in spreading innovation to patrons.

The magic of innovation is all about being ready to leap in and take on all kinds of challenges as they are identified. With the creation of the Digital Materials Group, we have helped to make this possible at Ela. We strive to remember that whatever our role is in our organization, it is far more important to be an advocate for innovation and help start conversations.

Spellcasting

If we really were wizards, we could wave our magic wands and library technology training would be effortless. Because we are mere mortals, we have to put in the effort. Training needs to be pertinent, thorough, and appropriate for people's skill levels. Because this training is, unfortunately, nonmagical, we have to accomplish all of these things within the constraints of our library and the needs of our patrons. This means technology training has to be dynamic, shifting, and fearless.

To accomplish this, we are constantly evaluating and revising our training offerings. By evaluating and observing our patrons' needs, we developed an appointment system for digital assistance, in which patrons can fill out either an online or paper request form for a one-on-one session with a librarian. The form asks patrons for their contact information, their general availability, the type of device they own, and the type of help or information that they are looking to receive. The form is then passed along to a digital materials trainer. Digital materials trainers are a mix of public desk and behind-the-scenes staff who have an interest in and aptitude for technology training. The appointment sessions range from basic instruction on using the library's digital downloading resources to working through technical problems the patron may be experiencing.

Our appointment system works well because we gain the opportunity to prepare patrons beforehand so they come in armed with all of the account information and hardware needed for a successful technology interaction. It also gives us time to gather information and prepare for the challenges that may be presented during the process.

By providing digital download appointments we give frontline staff support when working with patrons who need assistance beyond what can be handled at a public service desk. Staff gain the confidence to attempt to assist patrons on their own. The appointments work as a safety net if frontline staff are unable to completely solve the problem or if patrons just don't seem to understand what is being explained. Once an appointment seems necessary, a staff member then addresses patron expectations by explaining the time frame, generally within one to two weeks, for the appointment.

In addition to traditional classroom-style sessions open to everyone, we also provide targeted training through the Digital Materials Group. Our trainers are willing to tailor presentations for key audiences, such as the English as a second language (ESL) classes, focusing on the digital materials and electronic resources that are of most interest to these groups. For example, Mango Languages has specialized ESL components working with the English learner's first language, such as Polish or Spanish, translated to English. We work with the ESL instructor to customize student training for use of the product, from the first step of signing into Mango, to creating an account, and then getting started with lessons.

Staff training is a key component to help staff embrace technology. Once staff members are enthusiastic, they are better at assisting patrons and promoting new services. Realizing the importance of this, we have approached staff training in a variety of ways. Depending on the product being taught, we offer brown-bag, lecture-style training sessions held over the lunch hour or pop-up minisessions where a trainer will show up in a department or at a public desk during slow periods to offer informal, hands-on instruction. Keeping an eye on staff needs and abilities is critical. Do they need hands-on experience? Do they need assistance in formulating their patron scripts? How do they learn best? We try to make encouragement and support constant and consistent. The success of staff training lies in being able to "mesmerize" or simply convince others to join in the journey in the first place.

Mesmerizing

Innovation wizards have the power to convince people to become technology advocates, users, and trainers. A key component of successful mesmerism is to provide an element of fun and to remind everyone of why this new innovative technology is right for them. The library is a clearinghouse for technology information for patrons and staff. Therefore, we want to turn staff, our most powerful communication tools, into technology users, which in turn makes them advocates. We want to get them excited and talking about our services, whether it is to patrons, volunteers, neighbors, or family members.

One recent initiative has been a yearlong, library-wide effort called "Let's Talk About Tech, Baby." Each month the library focuses on a specific digital resource or service. The promotion is geared toward both patrons and staff, but for staff there are extra elements of fun. We try to play to our staff members' overall competitive nature and came up with a simple contest. Each time a staff member uses, talks about, learns about, or teaches the specified electronic resource, he or she is given a raffle entry for a small monthly prize. The end-of-the-year grand prize is drawn from all of the entries over the eleven months. Our objective is to give the staff incentive to stay involved in the initiative and encourage them toward personal bests of exploration and communication.

The initiative is coordinated and spearheaded by the Digital Materials Group. Because this group is made up of staff from all departments, we have a better chance for success with buy-in and involvement. Each department also has a voice in the support of technology and the development of promotional and educational pieces that are engaging, instructive, and user-friendly.

As part of "Let's Talk About Tech, Baby," there are monthly staff training opportunities with brown-bag, lunch-hour discussions and pop-up learning opportunities. We also hold fun events, such as Mango Mondays with mango treats for staff during Mango Languages month. The month we focused on the e-book resource Freading, helpful hints and a list of potential great Freading Friday reads were sent out to staff and posted on the library's Facebook page.

For patrons, we also look for ideas from the wider world that we can adapt and embrace at the library. At a trip to Starbucks, we found business-card-sized announcements for a free music download of the month. We adapted this to promote our Free Tunes by Freegal service. We created a series of a half dozen cards featuring various artists with the instructions for downloading free music from the library on the back of the cards and the artists' photos or album covers on the front. Networking with other libraries is also a source of inspiration. After seeing how a few libraries were using Facebook, we started a "Music Monday" post in which, every Monday, we post suggestions for weekly Freegal music downloads.

Maintaining openness to new ideas and a willingness to explore are powerful tools in the successful promotion of innovative projects. But we must also find ways to care for innovation and maintain projects after the shine has worn off.

Care of Magical Innovation

Our library will take leaps of faith when adopting new programs and tech-nologies. We took a leap starting our e-reader circulation program when our patrons expressed that they wanted an opportunity to do more than simply have a five-minute "test drive" of devices while at a store.

We wanted to keep things simple. Our first round of e-readers included all the original Nooks, and the program was a giant success. During our first year we could not keep them on the shelves and had a long holds list for every device. We augmented the classic Nooks with Simple Touch Nooks, when those came out, as well as some Nook Colors for the Children's Department. Again, Nooks could not be found on site and deep hold lists were generated. At the time, we could purchase one book and push it out to six Nooks, which made frequent updates with popular titles an easy task. Two years after the program started, however, it ground to a sudden halt with the announce-ment from Barnes & Noble that titles were now going to have to be one book to one Nook for institutions. This created a problem. We had so many Nooks. How would we be able to afford new titles for all forty-plus of them?

The Barnes & Noble policy change raised another important question: Were people still checking out the Nooks to test e-readers or because we now had popular titles (e.g., *The Hunger Games*, *Divergent*, *The Help*) on them? The only way to answer this question and move forward with the e-reader lending program was to do a more formal evaluation. The program statistics had spoken for themselves for most of the life of the program, but even before Barnes & Noble's announcement, we had noticed a decline in checkouts and wondered about causality. We all had theories, but no data to back them up. We decided to survey our patrons. The questionnaire we designed was available online through the free website SurveyMonkey (www.surveymonkey .com) and on paper in the library. SurveyMonkey made it easy to compile our results. The combined paper and electronic statistics showed an almost exact fifty-fifty split between patrons who wanted to check out an e-reader to try a new device and patrons who just wanted the books the devices contained.

The data we gained informed how we altered our device lending program while accommodating Barnes & Noble's new requirements. The Children's Department staff decided to focus on only their tablet-like Nook Colors and divided those into genre- and age-based sets. They also added iPads loaded with age-appropriate interactive books and apps, from Don't Let the Pigeon Run This App to many titles from the Toca Boca interactive suite. These iPads check out for one hour to Ela cardholders over the age of twelve, and they must stay in the library. Despite these restrictions, the iPad program has proven to be very popular.

For adults, we cut out all of the classic Nooks we had been circulating, as they were no longer in production and would not serve any patrons looking to try out devices before buying. Then, we weeded our Nook collections down to the most popular books for the remaining Simple Touch Nooks. This addressed the needs of the patrons who were checking out the devices for content alone and didn't care about the packaging. With the rising dominance of smart phones and tablets, we are still considering and gathering data on how to best approach providing multiple devices for patrons. Having the survey data to back up our decisions helps to quell any concerns about the changes we've made and will continue to make to the program. While we started this program with a leap of faith, ongoing feedback is helping to keep it relevant.

Conclusion

We hope that by sharing these lessons, we'll help make the work of library innovation attainable. Remember to communicate with staff and patrons every step of the way as you forge ahead, even if you aren't exactly sure where you are going. Use the tools at your disposal to analyze and evaluate where you are in order to help you on the path to discovering where you need to go. Until we get that actual magic wand or crystal ball, these are the lessons that all librarians can use to become innovation wizards.

5

Innovation Boot Camp

A Social Experiment

Robin Bergart and M. J. D'Elia

In 2010, we ran an experiment in our library called Innovation Boot Camp. We brought together eight library staff members to explore the meaning of creativity and innovation in the workplace and to discover whether we could boost our creativity through deliberate practice.

Over the course of ten weeks, we explored and tested different approaches to thinking and behaving more creatively, flexibly, and playfully. We used musical instruments, modeling clay, props and costumes, movies, board games, storytelling, and numerous other media to draw, build, improvise, and imagine a different kind of library.

Innovation Boot Camp (IBC) went viral, and we have since run miniversions of our program at several libraries and library conferences throughout North America. The University of Guelph (Ontario, Canada) Library is a member of the Association of Research Libraries and serves a student body of approximately 17,000 undergraduates and 2,000 graduate students. There is one central library on campus supporting all departmental programs, including one professional school, a veterinary college. We have found that the IBC program has had appeal in smaller community colleges, professional associations, and other types of organizations as much as it has in comparable-sized academic libraries.

This chapter describes the origins of IBC, what it looked like, and what we have learned about innovation in libraries from this experiment.

Origin Story

IBC was born out of frustration and skepticism at a time when our library was undergoing a major organizational shift. We were moving from a liaison librarian model in which librarians worked quite independently to a model of functional teams. The old ways of doing things were being dismantled, but new modes of working had not yet been established. Innovation was a core value described in the vision statement of our new organization:

> The library as an organization values and fosters innovation. We, as library staff members, are always seeking new and better ways of serving and working with the university community. We think creatively, embrace change, and take risks. We empower individuals, foster collaboration, and build teams with the capacity to discover, create, and act on opportunity.

Arguably, the library was embracing change and risk in a big way, but some things stubbornly stayed the same. We continued to sit through numerous meetings every week where little was accomplished except planning for future meetings. Ideas were collected to make our library a better place for our users, and these ideas would sputter out in committees before they could ignite. The organization was changing, but as individual library staff members, we didn't know how to think differently, experiment, and take risks.

By pure chance, both authors of this chapter started reading *The Ten Faces of Innovation* by Tom Kelley (see Selected Readings), a book about how IDEO, an international design firm, draws out the strengths and talents of its workforce to stimulate a creative and productive organization. Each "face" is a portrait of a particular set of skills, talents, and ways of thinking. For example, the Storyteller is strong at communicating ideas and the Director sees the big picture and delegates tasks appropriately. As the book argues, a team whose members include all ten faces of innovation is a productive, energized, and innovative team. M. J. identified strongly with the Experimenter face of innovation—the person who turns ideas into tangible products and services through iterative experiments and prototypes. Robin saw herself in the face of the Cross-Pollinator, who looks for the connections between seemingly unrelated ideas, things, and even people to create something new and unexpected. This book spurred us on: Could our library become more like IDEO? Could we learn to be more spontaneous, take more risks, and defy the stereotype of the slow-moving academic library?

With the chutzpah that comes with naïveté, we developed an innovation curriculum inspired by each of the ten faces in the book and pitched it to our administration. To their great credit, they gave us the green light, along with a small budget, and IBC was born.

Boot Camp as Metaphor

The name Innovation Boot Camp turned out to be an apt metaphor for what we were trying to do. On the surface, the name is an oxymoron. The word *innovation* evokes creativity, spontaneity, and freedom to tinker. *Boot camp* suggests discipline, order, rigor, and even pain. By linking *innovation* with *boot camp*, we serendipitously learned more about the challenge we had set for ourselves. Could innovativeness be developed through discipline and training? Is an academic library an organization that can embrace risk and change as well as continuity and stability?

The more we talked, the more questions we had. What could we change in our environment to draw out our colleagues' natural creativity, as well as our own? Are we all innately creative, or is there such a thing as the creative type? What does individual creativity look like compared to creativity generated in a group? What does it mean to be an innovative library?

The boot camp concept also served us well to stir up interest in our program. We dressed in army fatigues and held a recruitment session to pitch our program to the library. We invited our colleagues to fill out an application, complete with playful skill-testing questions (e.g., "Complete this drawing by incorporating the shapes and lines provided"), and awarded spots in the boot camp to six of the applicants. (The skill-testing application was a red herring; we selected all applicants whose participation was supported by their managers.) We notified selected applicants by issuing them each a boot camp kit bag containing all the gear they needed for the program. The items inside the kit acted as teasers for each boot camp activity, designed to intrigue and delight. The kit included, among other things, a notebook, modeling clay, small musical instruments, three beanbags, hot chocolate, and a black tie. We even provided metal dog tags stamped with "Innovation Boot

Camp." The unsuccessful applicants received a military-like rejection letter accompanied by a consolation lollipop (message: "Sorry, sucker!"). All of this was taken in the spirit of playful good fun with which it was intended.

We explored and exploited the boot camp metaphor throughout the program, stressing the importance to our new recruits of being on time, completing their assignments, and committing fully to the spirit of the experiment, an experiment in training for innovation.

The Curriculum

In this section, we lay out the rationale behind the curriculum with a few examples from the IBC sessions. Details of the full curriculum are available on the *Innovation Boot Camp* blog (http://innovationbootcamp.wordpress.com).

IBC convened for three hours on Friday afternoons for ten weeks. The new recruits came from many different staff groups and teams in the library, including librarians, library assistants, administrative support staff, professional staff, and a co-op student. Our library is the central library at the University of Guelph with approximately 100 staff members. As it turned out, most of the members of IBC did not know one another well and had not worked closely together in the past. The fact that we had little history with one another and that we were a diverse group with respect to skill sets, years of service in the library, and perspectives on the organization worked to great advantage. As *The Ten Faces of Innovation* suggests, group diversity is essential to innovation. Diverse strengths, talents, and perspectives encourage groups to tackle problems from different angles. Interesting, exciting new ideas arise when different disciplines and perspectives mix and intersect. The fact that most of us did not work closely together outside of IBC meant that we did not have preconceived ideas about one another and we were able to grow together as a new team.

Our first meeting was devoted to building a group identity and setting out the expectations for the program. We did not reveal the full curriculum to the recruits, partly because we had not yet filled in the details ourselves, partly because we wanted the program to evolve organically. We also wanted to provoke curiosity about what was to come, and as much as possible, we were full participants in the program working alongside the recruits.

We reiterated the experimental nature of IBC and the importance of coming to each meeting with an open mind and willingness to try new things and, perhaps, fail along with us. We stressed that IBC was not intended to directly address specific work issues in the library but to develop new habits of thinking and creative approaches to problem solving. We shared some of the questions about deliberately nurturing a culture of innovation that had stimulated the idea for IBC. We also committed to spending time on a guided written reflection exercise after each weekly meeting.

Our first group activity involved simple improvisation games. The foundation of improvisation is "saying yes" to people around you. It is about "accepting an offer" from a colleague and building upon it, rather than jumping to criticism or cynicism. These games can be uncomfortable and even scary for newcomers to improvisation, but they quickly build trust and camaraderie in a group.

Our second activity was the 100 Idea Brainstorm. We placed a vase full of giant, colorful lollipops (candy would become an important element of IBC) in the center of the table. We tied a note containing each of the rules for successful brainstorming, as found in *The Ten Faces of Innovation*, to each stick. After discussing these rules (e.g., "encourage wild ideas" and "defer judgment"), we had a short period of time to generate 100 possible names for our IBC team. What this activity demonstrated is the importance of setting out clear expectations as well as strict limits for problems. The problem was what to call our team. The expectation was to generate a minimum of 100 possible names within a very short time period. This time constraint pushed our team to focus intently on the problem and to encourage one another to build on one another's ideas. As for the lollipops and subsequent candy-fueled sessions, we thought the sugary treats would add to the anticipation each week, and providing them became our own private challenge of how to connect different kinds of treats to the theme of each session. The reflection exercise for homework after our first session was to consider the meaning of innovation and imagine what a truly innovative workplace would look like.

The following weeks were devoted to one or two faces of innovation per session. Each session began by sharing the personal written reflections on the previous week. We believed it was very important to balance the hands-on activity of the Friday afternoon sessions with time to reflect on the questions about innovation we had set out to investigate. We wanted all the members of IBC to think about these questions individually and then build a shared understanding in the group.

After a discussion of our reflections, we introduced the new session's face of innovation with a five-minute overview of the key skills and strengths of that particular face. This was followed by short warm-up exercises that we called the "mind stretch." These exercises provided further insight into the perspective and mind-set of the session's face. They also served to set the tone for the session and helped us to make the transition from our regular workday into the world of Innovation Boot Camp. They were a reminder to get into a mode for experimentation, risk taking, and thinking about problems in new ways. Finally, we developed a main activity each week as an opportunity to explore the session's face in greater depth.

One of the most elaborate and enjoyable main activities occurred the week of the seventh face of innovation: the Experience Architect. The Experience Architect creates a physical environment that supports and promotes creative thinking. He or she pays attention to the details that contribute to meaningful, authentic, and memorable experiences. One of the ways creativity is encouraged in organizations is by providing the materials to explore new ideas with plenty of whiteboards, comfortable chairs and cozy nooks, spaces for colleagues to easily bump into one another, as well as plants and natural light.

By this point in the program, the IBC group had really come together as a team. Our individual strengths had been drawn out during the previous weeks' activities and there was a great deal of goodwill, support, and trust in the group. The recruits were told to take the black tie out of their kit bag. They were paired up and told they were to pretend to be architectural firms competing for a contract in the library. The contract was to build a new space for graduate students, faculty, and visiting scholars to meet and exchange ideas. They had a set amount of time to draw up the architectural plans and prepare a short pitch. An additional element of the challenge was to work on the architectural drawings in a student study area of the library. The purpose was to step into our users' shoes and discover how these spaces enhanced or detracted from their work. The architects were instructed to return wearing their ties.

While they were gone, we transformed our regular meeting room into a formal, black-tie reception, complete with hors d'oeuvres, music, and a podium set up for the pitches. We set up an easel to display a unique logo for each architectural firm, which the architects stood beside when they made their pitch. Each architectural firm's pair of architects presented exciting and imaginative concepts for this new meeting space, and they did so in an engaging and entertaining fashion.

The reflection exercise for this session was to consider how the study space they had used to draw up their architectural plans affected their work. How important is one's surroundings to the quality and creativity of one's work? Once again, this activity showed us what was possible to achieve when the right elements are in place: a clear goal, freedom to play and experiment, trust in one's colleagues, openness to take risks, and the constraint of a tight deadline.

Outcomes

In Innovation Boot Camp, we set out to explore what it means to be an innovative library and to discover whether or not we could teach ourselves to become more innovative thinkers through deliberate practice. On a personal level, IBC was extremely gratifying for us as creators. We certainly did not anticipate that IBC would have a life beyond the ten-week program, nor did we foresee that the concept of deliberately exploring innovation would strike such a chord among our colleagues at other libraries. In the years since this experiment, we have had time to delve into the literature on innovation, reconsider these questions, and share our boot camp experiences and findings at many different libraries and conferences.

Some of the activities and challenges we planned were more fruitful than others as far as exploring innovation at work is concerned. We all agreed that the Experimenter, the Cross-Pollinator, and the associated activities we created for each were most relevant and meaningful for our workplace. The Experimenter taught us to "work with our hands" by creating tangible prototypes to complement the usual way we brainstorm ideas (by talking and writing on flip chart paper). The Cross-Pollinator persona encouraged us to look outside the library world to find new ideas. For this session, we challenged ourselves to consider how our library could be more like a submarine, summer festival, or tattoo parlor. The crazy connections we made helped us think about the library in brand-new ways.

On the other hand, some of the faces in *The Ten Faces of Innovation* seemed less relevant for our library setting and the associated activities felt like more of a stretch to understand how they could boost our creativity at work. The Caregiver was probably the least successful of our sessions, likely because we struggled to come up with concrete, relevant activities to illustrate it. Despite some of our missteps, Friday afternoons in IBC became a much-anticipated time for all of the participants.

An experiment like ours had potential to fail or, worse, to backfire. Participants might have felt that they dedicated many hours to practicing innovation only to return to their usual workplace without the power to make changes. Staff who did not participate in the experiment might have been skeptical about its value and resentful of the time their colleagues escaped from "real work" in order to "play around." To the extent that we worried about possible negative outcomes, we were insistent from the outset on framing IBC as *an experiment* whose value and potential was yet unknown and unproved. Staff who were not comfortable with this ambiguity chose not to participate. As creators of the IBC concept, we situated ourselves as full participants in the program, right alongside our "recruits." We were all in this experiment together and were all taking a risk that it would all be a waste of time, create resentments, or lead to frustration or disillusionment. All of these possibilities are part of risk taking and experimentation. We felt very strongly from the beginning that we were in need of new ideas and ways of doing things in our library, and that change implies risk and the risk itself is worth it. We were very grateful that our library administration was willing to support our experiment by lending precious staff time and energy to the project. We were also very grateful that a handful of our colleagues were willing to come along with us on this journey and trust that it would be challenging but worthwhile. It is far easier to take the safe and very understandable decision that we simply can't afford to "play." In the end, as cliché as it sounds, we feel we can't afford *not* to play. Otherwise we remain stagnant and become truly irrelevant.

Innovation Boot Camp did not have any calamitous outcomes; nor did it positively change the culture of our library in dramatic ways. Nevertheless, several specific, felicitous outcomes are listed here. Four years have passed since we conducted this experiment, and we continue to see examples of creative approaches to work that our colleagues trace back directly to IBC:

- The participants highly valued the opportunity to step away from the usual work routine, to explore ideas through experimentation and play, and to devote time to getting to know one another as colleagues. Play was no longer seen as frivolous or counterproductive but as an important element in generating ideas and building goodwill.

- Creating a special space to play and experiment was just as important as setting aside a special time. For IBC, we tried to create a different environment to suit the activities each week. As mentioned, one week the room was set up to host a black-tie reception; another week we set up a tent and gathered around a "campfire" to explore the tenth face of innovation, the Storyteller. These sometimes elaborate settings primed us to think differently, and we all began to notice how important our environment is to our ability to feel creative. Even though we could not always transform our environment so radically, we began moving chairs and tables around in regular work meetings to help us step outside the usual ways of seeing things.

- Participants were surprised by the creative energy that emerged in the group. Some had expressed prior skepticism about the idea that creativity could be a group experience, but we learned that a team of diverse individuals can generate surprising ideas and insights. Many of us who experienced IBC are now more open to our colleagues and deliberately seek out different opinions and perspectives for our work projects.

- In the library, we most often communicate ideas through spoken or written words. We found it liberating to experiment with expressing our ideas physically through building models, drawing, and role-playing. We were all surprised at the unique ideas that emerged when we constructed tangible models. Physical activity seemed to boost our mental activity, too. Since IBC, we and our colleagues have incorporated a variety of hands-on activities into regular meetings and brainstorming sessions, using LEGO bricks, paper dolls, personal trading cards, and a variety of other materials.

- Strict time limits on accomplishing tasks, like brainstorming 100 ideas in twenty minutes, focused our attention. Insisting on incorporating certain objects into our building models boosted our lateral thinking. In short, we discovered that deadlines paired with other limitations actually boosted our creativity. We began to reframe constraints as enablers to creativity. This has carried over directly into the workplace.

- Participants noted that they may not have bought into IBC as readily if it had been a program conceived and implemented by external consultants. The fact that the creators of IBC were colleagues who understood our library environment as insiders was more important than the fact that we had no special training or expertise in innovation.

IBC was conceived as a "skunk works operation"—an experiment that operated outside of the regular library work of the participants. These efforts have been positive but, in the end, limited. We strongly believe (and the literature on innovative organizations supports our belief; see Selected Readings) that a culture of innovation and risk taking must be modeled, encouraged, and facilitated by the organization's management team. Library management needs to enable, reward, and model risk taking and experimentation. Management must invest in new ideas; demand experimentation, assessment, and iteration in its services; and ensure the physical environment can support playfulness and creativity. New ideas must be encouraged from all corners of the library, irrespective of one's position or status. This is the only way a library can truly support and implement innovative change in a sustainable and wide-scale way.

We think that IBC has shown that an organization can become more inclined toward creativity and innovation through deliberate practice, and a library that takes this seriously embodies this in its management practice through action and reflection. The IBC experiment taught us to be more open to one another's ideas and insights and underscored the importance of a diverse team of talents and perspectives. It taught us the value of playfulness, experimentation, and taking a variety of approaches to problems.

Innovation has become a bit of a buzzword in libraries as we seek to redefine our purpose and value for our users. However, what innovation looks like in a nonprofit service organization like an academic library is not always obvious. While IBC revealed a great appetite for innovation in libraries, we think that the real need is not innovation per se, but the good, old-fashioned library value of user-centeredness. We learned this from the very first face of innovation in IBC: the Anthropologist. The Anthropologist is the great observer of human behavior. In the library setting, the Anthropologist pays close attention to how users search, study, collaborate, and generally interact with one another and their environment. The Anthropologist is looking for the pain points—the areas where our library impedes our users from effectively accomplishing their goals—and suggests creative solutions to overcome those impediments. This is where the potential for innovation lies.

Libraries do not need to hire creative geniuses, nor do they need to develop new and shiny products and services to remain relevant. Innovation Boot Camp showed us that the heart of innovation is in constantly asking, "Why do we do things the way we do?" and "How can we improve the lives of our users?" An open mind, an unquenchable curiosity, and empathy for our users are really at the heart of the matter in order for libraries to be more adaptive, nimble, and transformative.

SELECTED READINGS ON INNOVATION IN THE WORKPLACE

Amabile, Teresa M. "How to Kill Creativity." *Harvard Business Review* (Sept.–Oct. 1998): 77–87.

———. "Motivating Creativity in Organizations: On Doing What You Love and Loving What You Do." *California Management Review* 40, no. 1 (1997): 39–58.

Brown, Stuart, and Christopher C. Vaughan. *Play: How It Shapes the Brain, Opens the Imagination, and Invigorates the Soul.* New York: Avery, 2009.

Castiglione, James. "Facilitating Employee Creativity in the Library Environment: An Important Managerial Concern for Library Administrators." *Library Management* 29, no. 3 (2008): 159–72.

Crossan, Mary M. "Improvisation in Action." *Organization Science* 9, no. 5 (1998): 593–9.

Deiss, Kathryn J. "Innovation and Strategy: Risk and Choice in Shaping User-Centered Libraries." *Library Trends* 53, no. 1 (2004): 17–32.

Dyer, Jeffrey, Hal Gregersen, and Clayton M. Christensen. *The Innovator's DNA: Mastering the Five Skills of Disruptive Innovators*. Boston: Harvard Business, 2011.

Gertner, Jon. *The Idea Factory: Bell Labs and the Great Age of American Innovation*. New York: Penguin, 2012.

Jantz, Ronald C. "A Framework for Studying Organizational Innovation in Research Libraries." *College and Research Libraries* 73, no. 6 (2012): 525–41.

Johansson, Frans. *The Medici Effect: What You Can Learn from Elephants and Epidemics*. Boston: Harvard Business Press, 2006.

Kelley, Tom. *The Ten Faces of Innovation: IDEO's Strategy for Beating the Devil's Advocate and Driving Creativity throughout Your Organization*. New York: Doubleday, 2005.

Kurt, Lisa, William Kurt, and Ann Medaille. "The Power of Play: Fostering Creativity and Innovation in Libraries." *Journal of Library Innovation* 1, no. 1 (2010): 8–23.

Leonard, Dorothy, and Walter Swap. "How Managers Can Spark Creativity." In *On Creativity, Innovation, and Renewal*, edited by Frances Hesselbein and Rob Johnston, 55–66. New York: Jossey-Bass, 2002.

Light, Paul C. *Sustaining Innovation: Creating Nonprofit and Government Organizations That Innovate Naturally*. San Francisco: Jossey-Bass, 1998.

Linkner, Josh. *Disciplined Dreaming: A Proven System to Drive Breakthrough Creativity*. New York: Jossey-Bass, 2011.

Madson, Patricia Ryan. *Improv Wisdom: Don't Prepare, Just Show Up*. New York: Bell Tower, 2005.

Magadley, Wissam, and Kamal Birdi. "Innovation Labs: An Examination into the Use of Physical Spaces to Enhance Organizational Creativity." *Creativity and Innovation Management* 18, no. 4 (2009): 315–25.

Mathews, Brian. "Think Like a Startup: A White Paper to Inspire Library Entrepreneurialism." VTechWorks, April 3, 2012. http://vtechworks.lib.vt.edu/handle/10919/18649.

McLean, Laird D. "Organizational Culture's Influence on Creativity and Innovation: A Review of the Literature and Implications for Human Resources Development." *Advances in Developing Human Resources* 7, no. 2 (2005): 226–46.

6

Building a Toolkit to Craft Your Instruction Program

The Virginia Tech Experience

Tracy M. Hall, Edward F. Lener, and Purdom Lindblad

An instruction toolkit offers an important means to facilitate the sharing of techniques, strategies, documents, links, and news related to instruction and assessment. While there may be a designated instruction librarian, the task of providing library instruction and information literacy often falls to many different individuals within an organization. Since this larger group typically has a wide range of responsibilities as part of their primary job duties, it can be highly beneficial to have a centralized place to collect and share information specifically related to teaching and learning. An instruction toolkit can take a variety of forms; the key is to find what works best for your situation and needs. Such a resource can be particularly valuable when training those new to instruction or as a refresher for those who teach infrequently. Building a toolkit can also help strengthen an instructional program and create a greater sense of shared purpose among those involved.

For reasons such as these, the University Libraries at Virginia Tech began the Instruction Clearinghouse Initiative website more than ten years ago. Initially conceived as an internal resource, the pages were available to only Virginia Tech library faculty and staff. As the clearinghouse developed and grew, it became apparent that others could also benefit from access to this information, so, with further refinements, the pages were made publicly accessible. During this period, the University Libraries also sought to build up a broader culture of assessment and support for teaching (Ariew and Lener 2007). Going forward, a new and reinvigorated library instruction toolkit will take on much of the role of the original clearinghouse webpages while utilizing current technologies to better support collaboration and virtual communities.

Virginia Tech's Library Instruction Toolkit

The impetus for the library instruction toolkit (LIT) grew out of a direct need. During the spring of 2012 the University Libraries' Research and Instructional Services (RIS) department director, Lesley Moyo, initiated a library-wide call for information literacy instruction volunteers due to a growing demand for instruction and a need to redistribute instruction responsibilities. This invitation was an effort to grow the instruction team pool and provided a twelve-week training program during the summer of 2012. Particulars of the training emphasized the unique aspects of library instruction and included readings and discussion surrounding learning theories, instructional design, lesson planning, and use of teaching technologies in the classroom. In total, ten librarians and library staff responded to the RIS call, and the New Instructors Cohort was established. Upon conclusion of the twelve-week summer training, cohort members were not expected to start teaching immediately but continued to foster their own teaching identity through observations, mentoring, and co-teaching opportunities. This transition emphasized the need for developing a more robust virtual community. Anecdotal and survey results indicated that "more time for engaging activities, with feedback from program leaders, would be a valuable addition to the training program" (Miller, Barb, and Hall 2013). Building a supported LIT would be one such way to vitalize this transition from training to teaching. Such an active platform would work to highlight continuing education topics and foster discussion and feedback between both participants and program leaders. Moreover, it would also provide a library of teaching and assessment materials and resources. It became apparent during this time that building an interactive, virtual community toolkit was essential for successfully moving forward with our instruction initiatives.

Benefits of the LIT

While the New Instructors Cohort remains one of the key influences behind the creation of the LIT, this transition to a new system was also influenced by two additional needs: first, the use of a more modern and interactive platform as compared with the original Instruction Clearinghouse (which we discuss in the following section, Planning LIT) and, second, the reinvigoration of an internal teaching and learning community with the University Libraries for the instruction program. This type of platform would be an added benefit to our community, working to assuage the somewhat ambiguous role of the teaching librarian. Claire McGuinness (2011) explores this phenomenon in her book *Becoming Confident Teachers: A Guide for Academic Librarians*, describing today's teaching librarian as "something of an outlier in library and information work," a role that "seems to have evolved and emerged independently, rather than been consciously developed and nurtured" (1). This discussion is further impacted by the lack of formal preparation in teaching. Scott Walter (2005) suggested that despite a long history of involvement in the provision of instruction, and the current demand for the kind of teaching that librarians can provide, "few librarians are ever formally prepared to teach as part of their professional education" (1).

In 2007, the Association of College and Research Libraries (ACRL) approved the "Standards for Proficiencies for Instruction Librarians and Coordinators," outlining twelve specific proficiencies, including such key elements as instructional design, presentation, and teaching skills, to name a few. Awareness and implementation of these standards for instruction librarians and coordinators pushed the necessary skills for today's teaching librarians within academic university environments. However, even with this push and the surrounding debates that arose, it is critical to remember that "librarians need to know how to teach in order to have their instruction and curricular suggestions met with responsiveness" (Wilkinson and Bruch 2012, 15).

We believe that the creation of an internal LIT can work to combat many of the potential disconnections teaching librarians have related to instruction. A toolkit is one way to help create a community culture of learning and provides a well-balanced and fresh approach to library instruction. The challenge many librarians feel to incorporate the perfect dose of creativity, application of unique resources, new learning technologies and trends, and active learning strategies requires both energy and renewed innovation. Additional challenges include attention to learning objectives, variety of faculty assignments, new student researcher needs, and the ever-persistent lack of time. An LIT helps combat time constraints and acts as a streamlined resource to cull, share, and generate ideas and to view past assignments and readings related to library instruction. It can also provide a platform for creatively sharing instructional resources to assist librarians to achieve their instructional goals.

Planning LIT

In recent years, the Virginia Tech University Libraries have made increasing efforts to support open access resources and software. Building on this philosophy of openness, the authors conceived of the LIT as a focused teaching and learning inventory and virtual community, designed and housed on a free and modern software platform, as a means to better assist and support a growing instruction program. While the existing Instruction Clearinghouse (IC) has met with great success, particularly in documenting the past twelve years of instruction practices and assessment theory, the underlying webpage software makes it difficult and time-consuming to update and is limited in its ability to support virtual collaboration and community. The founding principles of the IC stress the significant gains made in sharing materials and fostering support within the community, but the limitations of the existing platform, coupled with the demonstrated needs of the New Instructors Cohort, made it clear to the authors that it was time for them to pursue more up-to-date, web-based options. After investigating possible alternatives, the authors found that WordPress (http://wordpress.org) would enable a variety of users to more readily contribute materials and blog posts, thereby creating an environment that should help to foster an interactive community of both established and novice instructors. We also appreciated its flexibility, potential for customization, and general ease of use.

During our evaluation process, which extended over a period of several months, two distinct needs emerged. The first arose from the recognition of the archival value of the information stored within the Instruction Clearinghouse. Particularly within the assessment pages, the IC documented significant changes within the libraries' policies and guidelines. It was decided that maintaining the IC as a digital archive of our teaching and learning activities and policies would provide long-term value. The second, as previously mentioned, grew out of the specific needs of the New Instructors Cohort, whose members were forming a community focused on creating and sharing instructional materials and experiences. A strategic remodeling and rebranding of instruction-related content to better support such efforts was necessary.

A critical examination of both the challenges and successes of the Instruction Clearinghouse demonstrated the significant historic value of the materials collected. Over a decade of library thinking around instruction goals, outcomes, and evaluation could be found in both the exemplar lesson plans and the assessment tools. We decided to more purposefully document current instruction theory and practice within the IC. Re-missioning the IC as a rich digital archive enabled the preservation of a reliable and known resource, while allowing sufficient time for the library to implement and launch a new platform for supporting instruction.

Virginia Tech is exploring networked learning, specifically encouraging the use of blogs in teaching and learning. As previously stated, we chose WordPress, which is both an excellent platform to support our goals and one which already fits within the landscape of teaching and learning at University Libraries and in the broader Virginia Tech community. Across our campus, students use blogs for networked reflection on both their formal and informal learning experiences. Within the library, blogging has connected us in previously unimaginable ways. The mysteries of what a particular position or department actually does have often now been illuminated through casual posts. Departmental blogs are aggregated into a single "mother blog," uniting the myriad missions and philosophies into a unified big picture. Building the LIT as a WordPress site fits in with a popular mode of communication within the University Libraries and serves as a unique space built by members of multiple departments who share a common thread of instruction.

While we desired a familiar, readily accessible platform, we did not want the LIT to look like "just another WordPress site." To build the LIT, we consulted with Alice Campbell, Digital Collections Archivist, and Andi Ogier, Data Science and Informatics Librarian, for WordPress training and advice on constructing digital collections. Several iterations of themes and

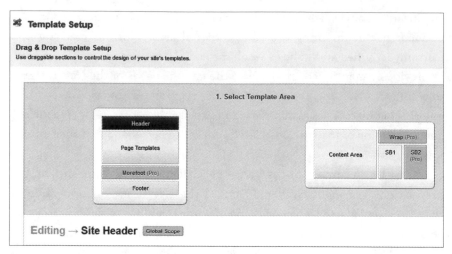

FIGURE 6.1

PageLines' Drag and Drop Dashboard

organization led to PageLines (http://wordpress.org/themes/pagelines).
A web design platform for WordPress, PageLines better adapts content to
look more like a dynamic website and less like a blog. The flexibility, ease of
customization, and low learning curve contributed to the selection of Word-
Press and PageLines over other possible platforms (see figure 6.1).

Another benefit of crafting the LIT within WordPress is the interactive
and collaborative features, such as an aggregated blog. Posts and comments
here can offer a way to expand and continue conversations around library
instruction concerns. In addition, the gallery and call-out features of Page-
Lines highlight posts of interest, new materials, or announcements (see figure 6.2).

In addition to the reasons previously mentioned, we selected WordPress
in part because we felt it was ultimately more sustainable than other platforms considered. The larger university hosts an installation WordPress,
indicating wide support for the platform. Excellent documentation for Page-
Lines and the broad community around WordPress simplifies the learning
curve, ensuring future librarians will be able to manage, refresh, and migrate
the LIT as needed. WordPress includes a variety of plug-ins to track site met-
rics, allowing targeted improvements to sustain use.

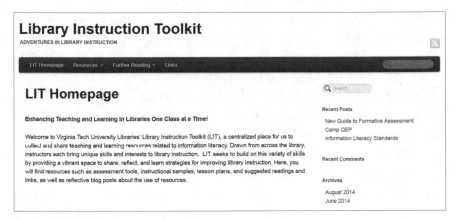

FIGURE 6.2

Library Instruction Toolkit—Initial Mockup

Implementation Ideas

The original IC relied on voluntary submissions, careful curation, and periodic reminders. Experience has shown that general calls for submissions are not as successful as individual outreach. As envisioned, the LIT relies not solely on voluntary submissions to gain material but can also serve as an interface for instructional materials, advice, and community support for future instruction cohorts. Face-to-face meetings reinforce the value of virtual supporting resources, as the LIT reinforces the value of in-person time. New Instructors Cohorts in turn pilot the creation of, submission of, and reflection on instructional materials.

The LIT can act as the major source of instructional community building within the cohort, and as new instructors complete training, the participants act as mentors for the next incoming group. Encouraging a mentoring model, we seek to maintain regular contributions from both current and past members.

Building and reinforcing the use of the LIT as a vital part of cohort activities would forge a foundational membership and encourage active use of the resource. The LIT can also contribute to an already thriving instruction community. For example, the library received two consecutive one-year grants from the Virginia Tech Center for Instructional Development and Education Research (CIDER) to run a community of practice focused on instruction and reflective practice and led by librarians. This group of library faculty and staff, which meets monthly and reads current literature and blogs about issues and opportunities in library instruction, is a natural partner for the LIT.

We should note here that unforeseen changes which have taken place with regard to personnel and in the departmental structure of the University Libraries have delayed the original time frame for the implementation of the LIT from when work began in late 2012. The recent creation of an all-new Learning Services unit within the library should help get plans for utilizing the LIT back on track and allow us to begin to fully realize its potential.

As the toolkit solidifies partnerships, further develops its role as virtual community platform for new instructors, and expands mentoring opportunities, it is essential to market the resource internally. A specific issue for marketing is addressing librarian worries about time, evaluation, and ownership. Thankfully, the mentoring program and the LIT itself significantly ease time concerns. Engaging with the LIT should be aligned with common habits and activities, and we designed the toolkit to accommodate these behaviors by enabling quick comments and creating multiples areas of access. Participants can submit materials through various means, including e-mail, Dropbox (www.dropbox.com), and writing or commenting on a blog post. In order to address concerns of evaluation, we focus on the assessment of student learning.

The LIT provides information about Creative Commons and author rights. By encouraging submitters to consider marking materials with copyright licensing, this approach builds a community of practice that aspires to best practices of information literacy as well as addresses concerns of attribution and ownership.

Future Directions

As demand increases for library instruction, strong considerations of scale, access, and continuity emerge around the LIT. The growing demand for library instruction has sparked an innovative training program. As outlined in earlier sections, the instructor cohorts draw employees from all departments within the library. The LIT can serve as a virtual hub, gathering into one central location blog posts, lesson plans, active learning exercises, and instruction materials, such as images, audio and video files, and presentations created and used by our community. The current focus of the toolkit remains on supporting the Virginia Tech University Libraries, uniting the CIDER instruction learning community, library reading groups, and the instructor cohorts. One potential avenue for future growth may be to collaborate with regional library instruction communities in which we participate, such as LEO: Libraries Exchange Observation (https://sites.google.com/site/librariesexchange/home), to expand the conversation and bring the benefits of a shared toolkit to a wider group of individuals.

REFERENCES

ACRL (Association of College and Research Libraries). 2007. "Standards for Proficiencies for Instruction Librarians and Coordinators." American Library Association. Approved June 24. www.ala.org/acrl/standards/profstandards.

Ariew, Susan A., and Edward F. Lener. 2007. "Evaluating Instruction: Developing a Program That Supports the Teaching Librarian." *Research Strategies* 20 (4): 506–15.

McGuinness, Claire. 2011. *Becoming Confident Teachers: A Guide for Academic Librarians.* Oxford, UK: Chandos Publishing.

Miller, Rebecca M., Christopher Barb, and Tracy Hall. 2013. "Library's Got Talent! New Library Instructors Discover Their Voices." Paper presented at LOEX 213, Nashville, TN. In *Library Orientation Series* no. 46. Ypsilanti, MI: LOEX Press.

Walter, Scott. 2005. "Improving Instruction: What Librarians Can Learn from the Study of College Teaching." In *Currents and Convergences: Navigating the Rivers of Change: Proceedings of the Twelfth National Conference of the Association of College and Research Libraries*, edited by Hugh A. Thompson, 363–79. Chicago: Association of College and Research Libraries.

Wilkinson, Carroll W., and Courtney Bruch. 2012. *Transforming Information Literacy Programs: Intersecting Frontiers of Self, Library Culture, and Campus Community.* Chicago: Association of College and Research Libraries.

PART III

INNOVATIVE OUTREACH

7

Get on Board with Community Needs

Ferry Tales, a Monthly
Book Group aboard a Ferry

Audrey Barbakoff

Ferry Tales may be the first library-sponsored book group aboard a ferry. This program has captured the imaginations of many and received local and national accolades for its inventiveness. I believe that it can stand as proof that anyone, anywhere, can innovate. The most exciting, impactful library programs and services do not have to strike in a middle-of-the-night flash of inspired genius. They can evolve from something you already do and know well. At its core, Ferry Tales is a simple, common library program: a book group. As I share the thoughts and methods behind creating and running Ferry Tales, consider how small changes and a fresh perspective might help your already solid programs grow into something amazing.

I launched Ferry Tales shortly after beginning a new position as an adult services librarian at the Bainbridge Island branch of Kitsap Regional Library in Washington. Before moving to the island, I had never been exposed to a community that relied heavily on ferry boat as a form of public transit. However, as Bainbridge Island is a thirty-five-minute sail from Seattle, it was immediately clear that a large portion of the adult working population commutes by ferry every day. I wondered how the library could improve service to this population. Riding the ferry myself, I saw many people reading but rarely saw the same faces in the library building. I decided to bring the library to them.

To support the many regular riders in my island community, I created Ferry Tales. Once a month during a busy commuter run, I lead a book discussion on board. The discussion lasts thirty minutes, much less than the standard book group; however, I find that this encourages the participants to use their precious minutes to really delve into the book, without veering off topic. In fact, the group is growing rapidly as our lively discussions attract the attention of other commuters. This group prefers for me to select the books, considering their interests but introducing them to authors or styles they might not normally read. I bring copies of the next month's title with me to each discussion for their convenience. To my pleasant surprise, I have found that although nobody needs to set foot in the physical library to participate in this group, most participants now come by regularly for books and programs or even just to say hello.

Although the group functions like a traditional library book club, the innovative location on board the ferry revolutionized the way the community perceived it. We are reaching passionate readers who never found the time to make it to the physical library, building community among riders of all ages and backgrounds, and garnering a surprising amount of local and national publicity that reminds people that the library is relevant, important, and even fun. In this chapter, I describe the process I went through to create and implement this program as a template for discussing library innovation in general. I share how I came up with the idea, won the support of my library system and my community, and continue to capitalize on the enormous possibilities it has opened up—and how anyone at any library system can do the same.

Start Outside

When creating a program, we often start inside our own organization; we think about what the library already does and then how that can be expanded to reach more people. However, such an inward focus can result in programs and services that are not as vital and relevant to their communities as they could be. As David Lankes said at ALA Midwinter 2012, in a speech available in full as a screencast on his blog, "What we really need to say is: 'What's the matter? How can I help you do that?' And [patrons'] first response will probably be: 'Well, this is what's the matter, but that's not the library's job. And that's our chance to go: 'Oh, isn't it? Why not?'"

In creating Ferry Tales, I started by looking outside the library, in my community. First, I observed the large number of ferry commuters in our community. Those observations were borne out by evidence; Washington State Ferries (2011) reports ridership of 4,026,194 on the Bainbridge–Seattle ferry in 2010, and Onboard Informatics (2011) estimated at the time that 27 percent of our workforce commuted by ferry. I wondered about the unmet needs these commuters might face. Though I often observed riders reading books, they usually did so alone and were not engaged in discussion. A commute can be boring and isolating, while a late arrival home means that most venues for socializing and building community in our small city are already closed. I suspected that a book discussion group would help turn the commute into a community builder, while introducing already passionate readers to new titles.

I made sure to ask community members if this idea truly met their needs. This is a critical step that we should never skip! Since for logistical reasons I approached this later in the process, however, I will address it in a later section to demonstrate how it fit chronologically. Ideally, you will do this as soon as possible, but it must wait until the idea has substantial backing from inside your library organization. This will unfold differently at each library, depending on its size, culture, and communication style.

Replicating the success of Ferry Tales is not about starting a similar program at your library, but about starting outside in your community. Think about its most pressing needs, and then consider how the library can tackle them. "Don't ask how the library can help," advised David Lankes (2012). "Instead, ask [patrons] what problems they need to solve, and ensure that they can."

Know Your Library's Process and Politics

Before I could go out and ask community members what they needed, I had to have the approval of my library administration. When you are excited about an idea, it can be extremely tempting to try to avoid this step. Playing the political game can be cumbersome and slow; your innovation might meet with resistance or outright rejection or proceed at a frustratingly plodding pace. Some of the steps you have to take might seem unnecessary or redundant. In short, this is probably not going to be your favorite phase. But it is absolutely worth doing right.

I went through my library's formal procedure for proposing a new program and found it extremely valuable. It won me the support of allies whom I would not otherwise have thought to seek out. It guaranteed system-wide exposure for my program so that other branches could benefit from my work. Best of all, it meant that I never had to worry that my program would encounter resistance down the line. I felt that I had the support of everyone, from my colleagues up through the library director, and that any problems I might encounter would be a shared concern we would address from the same side.

Kitsap Regional Library has a standardized project request form to fill out prior to starting a new, innovative program. The form forced me to articulate in very concrete, concise terms how Ferry Tales would support the library's mission and vision plan. Although this did not result in any significant changes to the program, it is a crucial factor in making sure the library's limited resources are allocated in ways that truly support the long-term goals for the community. Furthermore, it helped me craft an excellent "elevator speech," a quick way to pitch the program's value not only to library administration but to partnering organizations and community members as well.

In addition, as a new librarian at my organization, I had limited understanding of how the political structure worked beyond my branch manager. Who is in charge of this budget line, that decision, these resources? Who is the informal force behind getting something done, even if it is not in his or her job description? I needed to identify stakeholders on the form and also ensure that the form was sent to the right people. Although this process was sometimes frustrating, it prepared me for many future interactions, large and small. I now know whom to approach for a particular question or concern, when something can be handled with a quick call, or when a more formal process is needed. Going through the process for one program made all my future programs run much more smoothly.

Even the best idea can die on the vine without the support of key people in your system. Navigating your system's formal and informal political process, regardless of your opinion of it, can help build support from the beginning. It creates a stronger program in the moment and also builds relationships for the ideas you will want supported in the future.

Find Partners and Advocates in Your Organization and Out in the World

None of this has to be done alone. As a society and perhaps as a profession, we tend to idolize those we consider to be lone innovators or "rock stars." However, your innovations will be more interesting, more relevant, and more lasting if they have the support and input of others. From the very beginning, find allies on the inside. They will share your enthusiasm, be your reality check, and help you craft the best possible program before you present it to anyone outside the organization. While you will find some of these supportive people through the formal process detailed in the previous section, do not wait until that point to share with your colleagues. Even as you begin brainstorming, involve a few trusted and respected co-workers. Ferry Tales began as an offhand conversation between me and my branch manager. It went through several iterations based on the feedback of my co-workers and manager, both before and after I submitted my project request form, and those same people were there to support me and remind me of its value when I felt unsure.

After I had a robust internal support group, I sought out potential community partners. I strongly recommend this for any significantly new service. Even if the official approval or support of a partner is not necessary for your program, seeking it out will forge a stronger, more vibrant service. Ferry Tales partnered with Washington State Ferries, a relationship that is now growing and expanding. The operations manager at Washington State Ferries understood the culture on the ferry in a deeper way than we did, even though our staff members ride the boat regularly. She knew which part of the boat would be best for a large, loud group, and which times of day would be most successful. Better yet, because we brought her on board early, she has been a consistent and enthusiastic advocate for onboard library services as they have grown and changed. Community partners have ideas and resources that you have not even imagined. They are invaluable.

Ask Your Community

Frequently, libraries do not ask our communities directly what they would like to see in a new program. After getting buy-in from my own organization and the ferry system, I could have simply started up the program and hoped for attendance. However, I wanted to hear directly from my community first, and Ferry Tales may not have been successful if I had skipped this step. I reached out via action research, and it resulted in some notable changes to the program. It also allowed me to engage possible participants before the program began.

Rather than simply assume my idea would meet commuters' needs, I began a community conversation by riding the ferry at several different times of day and days of the week and talking with commuters. I created a small survey asking riders if they would like to participate in a book group and, if so, what they would like to read. This step was extremely important for Ferry Tales, and I believe it would be equally valuable for any library planning a new, untested program. For example, these discussions taught me that the needs of commuters in the morning are very different from those of commuters in the evening, even if the riders are the same people. I had originally planned a morning group but quickly learned from the morning riders that they wanted peace and quiet to start their day. On the return commute in the evening, however, they were very enthusiastic about the idea. Of equal importance, this interaction helped me develop a pool of interested riders in advance of the program, ensuring a substantial group from our very first meeting. Word of mouth was bringing in interest long before our formal PR (public relations) launch.

Although I was not comfortable approaching the public until my library system and partner organization were fully committed, you might approach your public earlier in the process. The best time and method to do this may vary based on the project and your community. The important point is simply to engage your community in some way. Ask community members directly if your service will be valuable to them. What you learn may be surprising and even necessary to the success of your program. In addition, the community involvement will create awareness of and excitement about your program before it even begins. By asking our communities what they need, rather than assuming we already know, librarians can create improved, vital, and deeply relevant programs.

Say Yes

Once your program is up and running, opportunities you had not considered will start to appear. Say yes to them. For Ferry Tales, the first opportunities were clear positives, with great results at little cost to us. For example, several local newspapers (Henry 2012; "It's Smooth Sailing" 2012) and the local television news station (Erickson 2012) approached us looking to feature the program. This type of opportunity snowballed for us; it felt like each time an article or feature appeared somewhere, another publication would notice it and approach us.

However, saying yes does not mean just accepting passive opportunities. Say yes actively. This requires an up-front investment of your time, possibly a significant one, but the payoff can be well worth it. For example, I wrote a short article about Ferry Tales for LibraryLab, a group within the American Library Association (ALA) that publishes library-related content online. The article appeared on Boing Boing (Barbakoff 2012), which in itself was a positive for our library, and it also brought Ferry Tales to the attention of *Shelf Awareness*, which featured the program as a "Cool Idea of the Day" (2012). That newsletter caught the eye of several well-known authors, who contacted me to ask if they could come and speak to my group. The exposure the program and the library received was wide, and well worth the time and effort. I am still seeking out ways to say yes actively for Ferry Tales and believe that these methods would be equally relevant for any innovative program. Write articles. Submit a proposal for a conference session. Propose a webinar through your state library or the ALA. Put in the time and effort.

Saying yes is challenging when you are faced with a suggestion for a change in your program. While it is emotionally difficult to let someone else's idea transform your program, seriously consider new ideas. For example, I was approached by Unglue.it, an organization working toward a digital rights management (DRM)–free model for e-book downloading, about hosting one of its authors on the ferry. We had never brought in an outside person for the program, and the logistics of coordinating both with Unglue.

it and with the author were a considerable investment of time and energy. The timeline was much shorter than is usual for my library's programs. Despite these concerns, I said yes. The experience was eye-opening, giving me a glimpse of what the future of Ferry Tales could be. We now regularly invite authors to participate.

Let It Go and Let It Grow

That partnership was the first moment I relaxed my own control of Ferry Tales. I had to allow other people's opinions, needs, schedules, and ideas to shape the program. That trend has continued and grown, for the benefit of my patrons, my library, and myself. No matter how much you love it, no matter how single-handedly you created it, do not hoard your program. Make sure as many people as possible are empowered to run it, continue it, and change it. You need to be free to go on vacation, accept a promotion, or shift your energy to innovating the next new program, without worrying that what you have created will wither away without you. Other librarians in my system have expressed interest in running Ferry Tales on the boats that serve their communities. I am glad to support them, but their programs will be their own, tailored to their own local needs. I am thrilled that this program can grow and spread without significantly increasing my workload.

As the program goes on, and you relax your hold on it, it will naturally want to evolve. Let this happen. The best innovations are often not the initial revolution but the incremental evolution (Stoiber 2012). In the wake of Ferry Tales' success, system-wide management became interested in expanding the service beyond the scope of what my individual branch can undertake. We are calling the new program Books Afloat. While Ferry Tales meets only once a month, Books Afloat will offer some kind of onboard library service once a week. By drawing on resources from around the system, we can find the staff to support regular author visits, instruction, book circulation services, and readers' advisory services in addition to the monthly book discussion. Because they can make executive-level decisions about our resources, administrators can easily implement the changes needed in our procedures and our technology to support circulating materials in a new location. Letting the program evolve into something larger, and in the care of a committee, will vastly expand the services we can provide. It takes the burden off of any one person to make the program sustainable.

I feel that this is my greatest success with Ferry Tales: it has grown beyond any one person. As long as it is a worthwhile service for our community and library, it will continue. Without this shift, no program, no matter how wonderful, will survive.

Conclusion

Ferry Tales has been lauded as an innovative program and garnered a significant amount of community support and media attention. It is growing into a much larger, wider-reaching service than I could have imagined when I started it. Yet it began simply as an established type of program—a book group—in a new space. What existing programs and ideas at your library might flourish if you reimagined them slightly, seeking out a new setting or a new partner? Important innovations in programming do not have to be earth-shaking revelations. They will arise just from thinking about your community's needs and how to address them. Start outside the library, thinking about the real needs in your service population. Rather than assuming you know, ask your community members what they need. Once you have an idea, help it flourish by knowing your library's process and politics, seeking partners inside and outside your organization, and saying yes even when the possibilities surprise you. Most important, be willing to let the program evolve once it is established. Let others take on responsibility and shape it with their ideas. This will ensure that your program is not only innovative, but sustainable.

REFERENCES

Barbakoff, Audrey. 2012. "Words on the Water." *Boing Boing*, September 20. http://boingboing.net/2012/09/20/words-on-the-water.html.

"Cool Idea of the Day: Ferry Tales." 2012. *Shelf Awareness*, September 21. www.shelf-awareness.com/issue.html?issue=1832#m17544.

Erickson, Anne. 2012. "A Book Club with a View." *King5 Evening Magazine*, November 29. www.king5.com/on-tv/evening-magazine/Ferry-Tales-181393601.html.

Henry, Chris. 2012. "Library Takes Book Club on the Water." *Kitsap Sun*, April 14.

www.kitsapsun.com/news/2012/apr/14/library-takes-book-club-on-the-water/ #axzz2MsXTbtwc.

"It's Smooth Sailing for New Book Discussion Group." 2012. *Bainbridge Island Review*, April 11. www.bainbridgereview.com/news/146984215.html.

Lankes, David, 2012. "Expect More: Our Most Important Conversation." *Virtual Dave . . . Real Blog*, January 22. http://quartz.syr.edu/blog/?p=1375.

Onboard Informatics. 2011. "98110 Zip Code Detailed Profile." City-Data.com. Accessed February. www.city-data.com/zips/98110.html.

Stoiber, Marc. 2012. "The Power of Incremental Innovation." *Huffington Post*, March 13. www.huffingtonpost.com/marc-stoiber/the-power-of-incremental-_b_1340705.html.

Washington State Ferries. 2011. "Traffic Statistics Rider Segment Report January 01, 2010 thru December 31, 2010." Washington State Department of Trans-portation. Posted January 10. www.wsdot.wa.gov/ferries/traffic_stats/annual pdf/2010.pdf.

8

A Librarian Walks into a Bar

Ben Haines and Kate Niehoff

A s of April 2013, the website TriviaReviews.com listed around 500 quiz events across the country, in communities of all sizes, and many more are likely happening without making it to the list. Why is this relevant to libraries? The generation of people now in their twenties and early thirties are in a unique place: they're the first to grow up with instant, online access to information, and they're the last to grow up with a library designed around reference questions like "Who was the twenty-first president of the United States?" Their idea of the library is stuck in time, regardless of how much the actual services and physical spaces have changed since they were young. Hosting an offsite trivia night can be a great way to tap into an ongoing cultural trend, reach out to this underserved audience, and change their perception of the public library. In addition, hosting a trivia night is firmly grounded in core library practices:

- Holding a library event at a local "hangout" is meeting the public where they already are, the same way that a mobile app or a remote-access database does.
- A trivia night is a unique PR (public relations) opportunity that can begin to build a new community of library supporters.
- Trivia asks participants to open their minds, learn widely about the world, and think creatively.

These goals are right in line with contemporary public library service.

In spring 2010, the Forest Park (Illinois) Public Library debuted its monthly trivia night at a local bar. The event was, at its outset, among the first of its kind for Chicago-area libraries. Over time, we learned valuable lessons about how to produce and sustain an innovative public program that continues to attract our target demographic of people in their twenties and thirties and reinforces community support of the library.

Step 1: Choosing the Venue

Choosing the right community partner is essential to the success of the event. An ideal location would be laid-back, noncorporate, and invested in the local community. Avoid sports bars and clubs; look for a community gathering spot with well-worn stools, darts, and cheap beer. If possible, find a place that doesn't have scheduled activities like ladies' nights, and choose somewhere that doesn't cater to families with children in order to focus on the target demographic. The venue should be reasonably easy for most people to get to, should provide enough tables and seating for the expected crowd, and should either have a microphone or provide a convenient outlet for a PA (public address) system to be plugged in.

Once an appropriate venue is found, approach them and offer a deal. By drawing in a crowd on a typically slow night (such as a Tuesday or Wednesday), a trivia night is an opportunity for the bar to increase revenue. Partnering with the library also represents a good public image boost, making the event a win-win situation for both parties.

Step 2: Designing the Event

The basic idea is simple: ask a set of questions, and reward the group with the most correct answers. The details, however, can vary enormously. The following outline presents some ideas on how to set up a successful event, but it should be seen as a starting point rather than a prescription. There's no right or wrong way to do it, as long as everyone is having fun.

Length and Format

The length of the event may be set by the host venue, particularly if there's some other entertainment scheduled for later in the evening. In general, though, around two hours is probably best. The next step is to choose the format. Some field research might be in order at this point: what are other trivia nights in your area doing? A typical setup might include six rounds of ten questions each. While multiple-choice questions are possible, and can be useful as tiebreakers, the standard format is a simple question/answer: for example, "Who holds the record for most successful three-point shots in the NBA?" Try to vary the subject of the questions; as with Trivial Pursuit cards, questions can cover history, geography, science, sports, art, or anything else. A range of topics makes sure that each team has an equal chance to excel.

The questions may require a little trial and error, both in format and in difficulty level. Questions that are too hard will quickly frustrate players, but easy questions won't produce the head-scratching and creative guessing that are part of the fun.

You can also include "novelty rounds," for example:

- *Picture round:* Players are given a printout or photocopy with a number of images (famous buildings, celebrity hairstyles, corporate logos, etc.) and must correctly identify the objects or people pictured.

- *Music round:* Players listen to snippets of songs and try to identify the title and artist, or the emcee could play a series of songs and ask the players to guess what the songs have in common (e.g., related to a topical political event, all by married couples, etc.).

- *Puzzle round:* Players are given a handout with a variety of puzzles to solve: anagrams, crossword puzzles, rebuses, and so on.

Novelty rounds can be longer, and they make for a nice break in the middle of the event. Participants can use the time to order drinks, visit the restroom, and so on. Also try to allow a few minutes between rounds for players to talk among themselves and critique their team's performance. This helps keep the atmosphere lighthearted.

Answer sheets can be as simple as blank pieces of paper or three-by-five-inch notecards, although printed sheets are common. Remember that participants are going to need pens or pencils and won't necessarily bring their own.

The Rules

It's a good idea to limit the size of teams to four to six players. This might split up large groups of friends, but a ten-person team competing against a team of two takes a lot of the fun out of the event. Each team should choose a name, and all teams should write their names on the answer sheets they turn in.

Other rules should be as simple as possible:

- No cheating (such as looking up answers on smart phones).
- Don't yell out the answers (because it ruins it for everyone).
- Have fun.

Lay out these rules at the start of every event, to prevent controversy later on. If there is a challenge to a question or a player who's clearly cheating, remember that the emcee is always right. Just like a deejay, the emcee has to be in control of the room, and his or her word is final.

Music and Sound

The clinking of glasses and chatter of people can make bars very loud places. If you want people to hear you as you explain the rules and ask trivia questions, you'll need to bring a PA system and microphone, unless the bar already has them available. Be sure to find an outlet and test your system before your first event, and take the time to ask the crowd if they can hear you throughout the night. It won't take long to find the optimal setting for reaching the ears of the farthest players while protecting the eardrums of those closest to the speakers. It is also a good idea to ask the bar if they can turn down the sound on their televisions for the duration of the event.

Playing music before and after the event will energize the crowd and set the tone for a fun, lively evening. It can also serve as an indication that the time for answering a trivia question is over. Decide beforehand how long you want the players to have to answer each question. Start playing music right after you're finished asking the trivia question, and stop it when the time for answering is over. Each group should turn in its answers shortly after the music stops. Set up your playlist ahead of time so that you're not wasting time searching for songs or switching CDs, and have an iPod or laptop ready so that you can hit play and stop at a moment's notice. Make sure to tailor your song choices to your audience members, and give them the opportunity to find the playlist on your website or Facebook page after the event. You can even link particular songs to the library's CD or downloadable collections.

Scoring

Be prepared to keep track of the groups' points as they earn them. A staff member should be ready to collect answer sheets and tally scores as quickly as possible. Make sure your system for keeping track of points is efficient. You can use a whiteboard to write down team names and add points to their scores after each round. One benefit to this is that players can see how far ahead or behind they are in the game. One drawback is that the staff member keeping score has to be a good mathematician who can add numbers quickly in a noisy, distracting environment. In order to save time and reduce errors, you can also make a simple spreadsheet ahead of time that will add numbers for you and have it readily available on your laptop or iPad.

Prizes

At a typical trivia night, the organizer collects a small fee from each player or team, then awards all or part of the cash to the quiz winners. Unless the event is being run as a fund-raiser, however, most libraries won't want to charge admission. That means it's necessary to get a little creative when it comes to prizes.

One simple way to handle this is to negotiate with the venue, offering to trade the increased business the library brings in for a donation of prizes. The venue's contribution could be cash, bar swag, alcohol, or whatever seems like it would appeal to most participants. Another option is for the library to provide the prizes out of its own budget or through donations.

In addition to a prize for the winners, offering a consolation prize to a low-scoring team is a good way to get repeat attendees. Letting the losing players select a theme round for the next event is a great incentive for them to come back. Other ideas might be to offer a prize for best team name, a spirit award, or an award for funniest incorrect answer, to keep the night moving and the crowd engaged.

Potential Expenses

Running a trivia night does not come without expenses. The following list represents tangible items you'll need to buy, if you don't own them already, to ensure a successful event.

- *Quiz books or question sets:* Owning a few books of trivia questions or buying packages of trivia questions will save you valuable staff time. You can also subscribe to online databases of quiz questions that are updated frequently.

- *Tech equipment:* If your library doesn't already own one, you'll need to get a portable PA system with a wireless microphone. You can find dependable, small PA systems for less than 100 dollars. You'll also need an iPad or laptop for keeping score, playing music, and keeping track of time.

- *Game supplies:* Teams will need answer sheets and pens or pencils. Pens and pencils often don't get returned, so be sure to keep a large supply on hand and sharpen pencils ahead of time.

- *Promotional materials:* Promotional materials, such as postcards that trumpet new programs and services, can be designed and printed in-house to keep costs down. For a little extra money, you can get pens or pencils made with your library's logo printed on them.

- *Prizes:* Prizes for the winning team can be as simple as a round of drinks from the bar. Most teams will be participating for the fun, so prizes are secondary. If you do choose to offer something more elaborate, don't be afraid to ask for donations. Local shops and businesses will often jump at the chance to promote their businesses by donating gift cards, tickets to shows, free meals, and more.

Step 3: Using the Right Staff

Unlike many traditional library programs, a trivia night is as much a performance as a presentation. "Performer" isn't usually part of a librarian's job description, so it's a good idea to choose staff members who are excited about getting up in front of a room full of people and having all eyes on them. A crowded bar provides a great opportunity to make small talk while also making connections, so look for staff members who are enthusiastic and knowledgeable about the library and its services. Good communication skills are essential, and conflict resolution is important, too: when a participant wants to contest a quiz answer, it's the emcee's job to turn that into a positive interaction rather than a shouting match. It shouldn't be a problem to find an authoritative source to back up a disputed answer, if necessary, but also remember that an extended argument isn't fun for the rest of the crowd. The emcee's judgment has to be efficient and final.

Age is a factor, too, but not having staff members in the target age demographic isn't a deal breaker; an outgoing personality with a knack for performance is more important.

The number of staff needed will depend on the size of the crowd and the number of questions in the quiz. At least two people are probably needed: the emcee asks the questions and engages the audience, and an assistant handles the music and scoring, collects answers, and generally keeps things running smoothly.

Step 4: Publicity

The first step in any marketing plan should be to determine the places where your target audience is likely to see your event mentioned. People in their twenties and thirties tend to be tech-savvy, connected with social media, and own smart phones and tablets. (See, for example, the Pew Research Internet Project at www.pewinternet.org.) This makes Twitter and Facebook obvious communication channels. Tweeting teasers for the event leading up to the date can build excitement, as can reminders on both the venue's and the library's Facebook pages. To reach people who aren't already followers, create a public Facebook event. This allows people to share the event with their friends even if they don't follow the library or the venue. If your community's target demographic is using Meetup.com or other online channels for events in the area, consider publicizing on those sites as well.

Because younger adults are notoriously averse to marketing speak, phrase these online pitches in conversational language. The popularity of trivia nights goes hand-in-hand with the rise of nerd culture. Embrace the new hipness of librarians, don't be afraid to be snarky, and remember that DIY (do-it-yourself) is now cool.

The community partner can also help market the event. Beer distributors will often provide bars with custom vinyl banners that can be used for advertising at the venue. If possible, make sure that the banner contains the library's name and logo. In addition, whatever channels the venue uses for its own marketing can be used to publicize a new event.

Step 5: Communicating the Library's Message

Unique outreach events aren't just a chance for librarians to let their hair down; they are PR events for the library. The return on investment depends on being able to deliver a clear message to the audience. To communicate effectively, make the event a part of the library's brand. Try to include the library's logo and URL on trivia night materials like answer sheets, pencils, picture round handouts, and so forth. The emcee should also work references to the library into his or her banter, maybe by gently making fun of library stereotypes. Remember, the goal is just to associate a fun experience with the idea of the library, not necessarily to list all your programs and services!

When you do promote programs and services to your trivia night audience, keep the messages brief and targeted to your demographics. A plug for a program followed by the URL is about as much information as you can hope to convey. Film screenings, special music or video collections, e-media, makerspaces, and tech labs are all good choices. While you certainly can't communicate all of the value your library has to offer during a noisy night at a packed bar, you can drive people to your website or social media pages for more information. Whenever possible, make the extra clicks worthwhile for your fans. For example, post the night's music playlist or the funniest answers, rather than just promoting the library. This sort of outreach is an opportunity to build community, not to be a platform for library announcements.

Step 6: Sustainability

Initially, the excitement over a new event might bring an audience back month after month, but eventually there will come a time when a trivia night stops being novel. How do you keep people interested? The most important way to keep people coming back to an event is to make sure everyone's having a good time. Pay attention to the crowd. Are there times during the quiz when people seem bored? What parts of the event are capturing people's interest, and which aren't? If attention seems to flag near the end of the quiz, it might be a good idea to speed things up by having fewer questions. If people keep getting up to go to the bar rather than listening to the questions, you can build in drinking time by having a picture or music round. Play around with the format. Different crowds respond to different things, and there's no harm in experimenting a bit before settling on a regular routine.

Talking to participants after the event is a great way to spread the library's message, but it's also the time when your audience gets to tell you what they liked, or didn't like, about the evening. Don't be afraid to ask questions, like whether or not the questions were too hard or if there is anything they would like to change about the format. Many participants will probably be regular trivia players and can bring in ideas from other events that you may not have considered. That said, take everything with a grain of salt. If the losing team tells you the questions were too hard, it's probably just sour grapes. Ultimately, it's up to you to define the character of your event, and that character should keep people engaged.

Step 7: Measuring Outcomes

Many of the benefits of nontraditional outreach might not be tangible. Even if a participant never attends another library program or never uses the library's services, seeing the library engaged with the community can make a difference in that person's support. Meeting library staff in a social setting also gives people the chance to learn names and faces, even if they'll never approach a reference desk. When a request for instructors, donations, or other assistance comes from someone familiar, it's much less likely to be ignored.

Quantifiable outcomes like attendance are important, but keep in mind that attendance can vary widely from month to month, as with any traditional program. Bad weather, good weather, a sports game, or a competing event can affect the size of the crowd. Just because one month doesn't draw good numbers, does not mean you've lost the public's interest.

Perhaps the most rewarding, but difficult to quantify, result of the Forest Park Public Library trivia night has been the way it's expanded opportunities for community engagement. The library is now hosting a regular bridge night, organized and run by a contact made at the trivia event. We developed new e-mail-blast publicity based in part on feedback from trivia participants. And one regular trivia night attendee has recently become the newest (and youngest) member of the library board. Much is made of the "elusive nonuser" in library circles. It's impossible to tell, of course, how many trivia attendees fall into this category, but the conversations that happen around this monthly event are often rare within the library building. We hear what the community really thinks and wants, and we can respond by innovating and adjusting our programs and services.

Conclusion: Make It Happen

While the traditional focus of the public library is on education, the trend over the past decade has been toward a widening of purpose. Libraries now also act as community centers, as sites for creative play and community engagement, and as curators of pop culture. Unfortunately, public opinion has been slow to follow these changes. Unconventional outreach and programming like a trivia night can be a great way to connect with the community. Over a couple of beers and some fun questions, you can show people the relevance of their local public library.

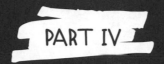

PART IV

INNOVATIVE TECHNOLOGY

9

Seizing the Opportunity for Innovation and Service Improvement

Cheryl McGrath and Brad Warren

We think it bizarre when something in the digitally networked world
does not mesh with something else, perceiving whatever it is to be broken,
in need of repair. This high degree of expectation is a powerful driver of
interoperability. (Palfrey and Gasser 2012, 28)

What happens when an opportunity presents itself in ways which are not anticipated or which occur from outside a person's normal frame of reference? In the case of the two examples outlined in this chapter, these innovations came about through the shared interest in making improvements by librarians in two separate institutions who were wrestling with the same issues at the same time. While the development of these solutions may appear to have happened through chance, they provide an example of recognizing opportunity and acting upon it when the moment presents itself. In this chapter, we outline two different innovation projects using the layers of interoperability to retroactively assess how the innovation was achieved. Both of these projects have at heart the desire to simplify services delivered to patrons, in a way that is effective from the perspective of both staffing models and patrons' experience.

Inscriptio: An Online Carrel Seating Reservation System (Cheryl's Story)

In the fall of 2010, I walked into the Privileges Office at Harvard and observed stacks upon stacks of paper. Thousands of pages were being collated into hundreds of packets for new carrel users at the start of the academic year; in addition, there were boxes of hundreds of plastic identification (ID) cards, costing three dollars per card. When asking the team more about the application process, I learned that we were not meeting the goal of a simple and effective service. The process was manual and involved an in-person application, extensive negotiations around preferred seating and availability, saved terms-of-use signature pages, secondary ID cards, and packets explaining policies and procedures that the team suspected were never read. There was no interoperability at the technological or data level. At the human level, I could hear the frustrations of the staff and patrons as the current process did not allow for effective communication: carrels without books on the shelves "looked empty" to patrons even though triple booked, and staff had a hard time convincing patrons their desired spots were unavailable.

While I was certainly asking questions, my main activities at this time were to observe and listen. Early on in my role, a senior administrator commented what a wonderful role the staff in Privileges filled, as they had jobs where they got to say yes to people all day, every day. Yes, you can come into the library. The gap between the perception and the reality was stunning. The stories I heard from staff were about all the instances of no. In order to protect the library space for students and researchers, staff said no to busloads of tourists and once refused entry even after a fully costumed mariachi band offered to serenade them in return for access. The staff knew they were right to say no; it was the discrepancy in perception and experience that we needed to bridge, and here was an opportunity to improve the process.

Days before, I had been online purchasing airline tickets, and as I stood among a sea of paper and a group of staff mentally gearing up for the fall semester avalanche of requests and negotiations, I was struck by the vast difference in what was essentially a similar process. I had been able to book a trip to Florida with an aisle seat on an exit row for leg room from the comfort of my own home. Why couldn't our patrons do the same thing for a study carrel? Shouldn't they be able to check carrel availability and then choose one near the collection relevant to their dissertation?

While I had envisioned a solution, I needed help to create the product. Harvard University Library (Cambridge, Massachusetts) had recently launched a program called Library Innovation Lab, funded by a grant from the Arcadia Fund. Accepted proposals would be teamed with developers from the Berkman Center for Internet and Society. I submitted two proposals, one for an automated carrel seating app, and another for an exit security app (more later on this). The reviewers requested more information on the exit security app and approved the automated carrel seating app. When Anita Patel, our assigned developer, arrived, it was time for the Head of Privileges, Ann-Marie Costa, and me to listen carefully to the staff to help Patel translate their requirements to ensure my flash of inspiration could become an effective tool to improve service. The team at Privileges had thorough and thoughtful feedback, and the development team listened, brainstormed, and built the app, and everyone tested the product.

The interactive carrel seating application, aka Inscriptio, successfully launched in the fall of 2011. What was once a time-consuming process involving an Excel spreadsheet, paper applications, and thousands of pages of carrel packet information printed yearly is now a streamlined online function. We estimate that this application will save five weeks of staff time and 800 dollars in supplies per year, which makes this a green initiative as well. Before the online reservation system, staff had no reporting mechanism for available or expired carrels but did have the challenge of explaining to patrons that even though the carrel they want is physically empty of books, it is reserved by four of their peers.

Eligible patrons are now able to apply for a carrel or hold shelf in Widener or Pusey Library via an online application. Once registered, they can navigate their way through floor maps of the libraries, showing which carrels and hold shelves are available. They can cross-reference availability with subject classification adjacencies, ensuring they are as close as possible to their research area of interest. Patrons can then choose a carrel, much like one chooses a seat on an airplane or train. After staff run reports on pending reservations and approve the patron, an e-mail is generated, sending the patron information on how to charge items to the carrel/hold shelf and any other relevant information, such as the combination for the carrel locker. Patrons assigned to a particular carrel can communicate with one another to schedule use times via a bulletin board built as part of the application. As patrons reach their chosen reservation end date, the application automatically sends an e-mail with renewal options. Staff can run reports on expired reservations so that the space can be cleared and made available for future use.

As the project was developed, staff were inspired to create a work-around, streamlining the process of charging items to carrels/hold shelves for staff and patrons. In the past, when patrons applied for a carrel, they received a separate library card allowing them to charge material to the carrel. Patrons then had to carry around two cards when coming to the library to engage in research. By populating the Additional Notes Field One in Aleph, our integrated library system, with a patron's carrel number and the pseudo-patron card number for the corresponding carrel, we were able to push that information to the loan screen in the patron details box. This eliminated the need for a separate carrel card. Patrons now show their Harvard-issued IDs at the Circulation Desk, and from there the staff copy and paste the carrel numbers so that materials are charged appropriately (Costa and McGrath 2011).

Our goal of a simple and effective service was now being met, and our interoperability functioning was at a high level—all because of the juxtaposition of booking an airline ticket online at the beginning of carrel season. Innovation doesn't have to be a brand-new idea; it can be taking an existing idea and reshaping it to improve outcomes.

Red Light/Green Light: Real-Time Circulation Data at Security-Monitored Exits (Brad's Story)

I met Cheryl at a conference not too long after I began working at Yale University in 2009, but it was the development of the Inscriptio carrel assignment software that started a closer collaboration. Yale University shares many similarities with Harvard in its clientele, decentralization, and unique problems. We, too, had a complicated manual process to assign and renew carrels that was difficult to maintain. This collaboration began when I visited Harvard and spoke with Cheryl's Access Services Team about their Inscriptio program. Aside from walking away with what appeared to be a good solution that could be adapted to our own situation, I also discussed with them other initiatives and problems, seeking technological solutions. One of these ideas in particular had to do with improving and speeding up the process by which patrons left the building. In both of our libraries, we had a pass-through security system that required a lengthy book and bag check by a security guard at each exit. Cheryl was consulting with Laura Morse, Director of Library Systems at Harvard, to revise her proposal for a technological improvement to submit to the Library Innovation Lab that developed Inscriptio. Her concept was to create a Red Light/Green Light app that facilitated security at exit points by scanning existing bar codes in lieu of date due stamps. I came away from our meeting thinking that (a) I wish Yale had a group like the Harvard Library Innovation Lab that would develop technological innovations in a similar way, and (b) wouldn't it be interesting to collaborate with another institution on a technological solution that could potentially be shared?

Toward the end of the year, while having lunch at the annual Access Services Conference in Atlanta, Georgia, we shook hands on each of us developing one of two separate technological improvements, each of which not only would be beneficial to our own users but also could possibly be adapted for use by the other institution. I agreed to develop the Red Light/Green Light system. I felt confident that it was possible to do this development based on the following factors:

- The exit procedure at the library was our number-one complaint by patrons.
- Unlike Harvard, we experienced the arrival of several tour groups for whom the library was a destination. During the month of July 2011, we estimated that we had over 18,000 visitors to the library by outside groups—literally busloads of tourists. It was critically important to shorten lengthy book and bag checks with a mix of students, faculty, staff, and tourists trying to leave the building at the same time.
- The library building was soon due to undergo renovations, which would be a perfect time to introduce these types of changes that were procedural as well as operational.

- The system would allow for a friendlier self-checkout experience by our patrons, which was an important development in the renovation.
- The system would pave the way for a green initiative to end use of date due slips.
- The system would have the potential to allow security guards to change their focus from the books in front of them to being aware of the people and environment within their line of sight.

I filed all of this away, spoke about the idea to my staff, and placed it firmly on the back burner, where most ideas either die or become irrelevant. However, this was not the case of agreeing to do something that could not be done but instead filing away this initiative, along with a host of other improvements, until the time was right for expansion and development. This time came just four months later while I was on paternity leave.

Although I do not advocate checking one's e-mail rigorously while dealing with a newborn, I did lurk online a bit to see what was going on while I was away on leave. About three weeks in, I had to respond. At the time, the guards were trained to look carefully at the due date slip placed in the back of each book to match the last four digits of the bar code with a due date that was sometime in the future. Any book renewed online would require having a new duplicate due date slip printed out by circulation staff so the person could leave the library without a problem. For books with short loans or books checked out from our consortial Borrow Direct service, this was a significant problem. An added difficulty was that printing a duplicate due date slip required staff-level permissions, and it was not long into my leave that we had a serious (and very noisy) complaint in which a staff member was not around to produce that slip and enable the book to leave the building. To my horror, the following solution was presented: get a due date stamper just for this purpose. At this point, I e-mailed the group, which included Library IT (Information Technology), about the idea of Cheryl's Red Light/Green Light system. To my great surprise and delight, it was developed internally by Library IT in conjunction with our Access Services Department and Library Security and up and running exactly five months later.

The idea behind the Red Light/Green Light system was, to quote Cheryl, "If the security team had a simple app that ran on a device attached to a scanner, they could scan each bar code in rapid succession and the screen would display a green check for go and red X for no-go. No-go would inconvenience the patron in that they would have to return to the circulation desk, but the many others in line would benefit. This would also improve the guard's interactions, as the onus was on the system and not them; the system indicated whether an item would be allowed to leave the building."

At Yale, we developed the Red Light/Green Light system in which the guards use a scanner attached to a minilaptop that scans the bar code and produces a green screen with the word "Pass" and a number count or a red screen with the word "Stop." The green or red designation is delivered via a website logging transactions by each exit desk (there are three), and responses are almost instantaneous. Any patrons with a red-screen scan are instructed to take the items back to the circulation desk. No patron information is gathered.

All decisions in the specifications of the system were geared toward making the process as simple and quick as possible for security staff, with the assumption that this would translate to an improved experience for patrons leaving the library. The initiative was led by our Access Services IT Manager, who managed the project, worked with our stakeholders (Library IT, Access Services, and Library Security), tested the system, and ran time trials with the system, both when it went initially into production and then three months after it was implemented. While there was some skepticism on the part of the guards about whether the system would indeed be an improvement, all stakeholders were fairly positive about the entire development and implementation. Highlights of the development included:

- Giving guards several test options for scanners allowed them to provide usability feedback.
- Optimizing the real-time lookup ensured that responses would be as close to instant as possible.
- Delivering this functionality on a simple to maintain and support interface (e.g., web-delivered) promoted ease of use.
- Circulation staff changing procedures to put duplicate bar codes on the front of every book checked out made it easier

for guards to find and scan the bar codes. It should be noted that this worked because:

- our existing procedures to send materials to our Library Shelving Facility required the creation of duplicate bar codes, so we already had some of the equipment; and
- we dropped the requirement for circulation staff to place due date slips in a holder in the back—they could just drop the slip loose in the back, a compromise that was viewed very favorably by circulation staff.
- Keeping a database of each scan allowed storage and quick access to the captured information: bar code number, date/time stamp, exit location, and pass/stop code.

The system was put into place in mid-August 2012. As we completed the second academic year of having the new system in place, we not only met our original goals of the project but also had some unexpected surprises. The system has been received well by the guards, with a marked decrease in the time it takes for book and bag checks at the exits. Other libraries in the Yale system have also expressed interest in having the system expanded to their locations, which would require a minimum of coding necessary for the expansion. The system, in combination with security footage and an alert guard, also aided in the identification of someone attempting to steal library materials. We plan to phase out due date slips and have built the infrastructure necessary to support expanded self-check services that went into production in August 2013.

By the time the system was in place and functioning as desired, some things had changed: Cheryl had a new position at a different institution, and I figured that I would wait awhile for Harvard to emerge from reorganization before contacting them again to see if there was interest in the system. Much to my great surprise, not only was Cheryl extremely pleased that we actually built the system, but there was interest at other institutions with the same problem. Harvard instituted this feature, branded as Secure Exit, in January 2014 at the Widener and Lamont Libraries ("Scanner Speeds" 2014). While the development of the Red Light/Green Light system and the subsequent sharing with other institutions did not play out as I had expected, its development has been a great success and we hope that this collaborative project can be of use to other institutions in the future.

Sometimes you have to wait for technology to develop enough to meet your innovation needs. Be patient. If you can identify and articulate the problem you are trying to solve, it will stay with you as you search for a solution. It took me almost ten years to figure out how to solve the problem that Red Light/Green Light solves. Initially my time was spent identifying the problem, then I just needed to wait for technology to catch up and present a viable solution. If "[t]he incentive to change is not yet high enough to overcome the inertia that develops in systems that are highly interoperable at the human and institutional layers" (Palfrey and Gasser 2012, 44), then it is hard to get traction with an innovative idea, no matter how well it might serve the institution and its patrons. An innovative idea that increases interoperability and meets the goal of simple and effective service may not be the right idea at your institution at an exact moment in time, but don't let that stop you from sharing the idea with others.

Seeing how other industries and other libraries handle their information sharing and throughput can help you better articulate what you want to improve in your own area of work. Your process of discovery can be as simple as visiting area libraries, going to other spaces on campus, or going into town where information sharing, storage, and collaboration are taking place to see what you can learn. Observe, listen, question. Soon you will be cooking up some innovations of your own.

REFERENCES

Costa, Ann-Marie, and Cheryl McGrath. 2011. "Inscriptio: Project Summary." *Weblogs at Harvard Law School*, October 28. http://blogs.law.harvard.edu/cmcgrath/2011/10/28/inscriptio-project-summary.

Palfrey, John, and Urs Gasser. 2012. *Interop: The Promise and Perils of Highly Interconnected Systems*. New York: Basic Books.

"Scanner Speeds Lamont, Widener Exit Lines, Improves Collection Security: Secure Exit Replaces Manual Review with Scanning." 2014. Harvard Library. Posted January 14. http://library.harvard.edu/01132014-1014/scanner-speeds-lamont-widener-exit-lines-improves-collection-security.

10

The "Eyes" Have It

A Digital Media Lab in an Academic Library

Pat Duck

Multimedia design center, digital media lab, makerspace, scholars' lab—there are many names for the ways that academic libraries are embracing a wider definition of the "library as space" concept, "where new and emerging information technologies can be combined with traditional knowledge resources in a user-focused, service-rich environment that supports today's social and educational patterns of learning, teaching, and research" (Freeman 2005, 3). While actively renovating and reinventing spaces for information/knowledge commons areas, the rationale for this movement is to provide an environment where students have access to equipment and space to experiment. The underpinning of this movement encompasses two key missions of academic libraries: to develop skills in information literacy and to encourage critical thinking among college students.

In recent years, the term *visual literacy* has been used to describe a crucial skill for twenty-first-century students who are routinely bombarded with information delivered in a specifically visual format. Although the term originated in 1969 and is attributed to John Debes, co-founder of the International Visual Literacy Association (IVLA), today visual literacy is seen as "a central component of liberal education" (Little, Felten, and Berry 2010, 44). With the introduction of the Association of College and Research Libraries' "ACRL Visual Literacy Competency Standards for Higher Education" (ACRL 2011) and the realization that "many of our students may not be critical readers of images and visual information," it is clear that libraries have an

obligation to embrace ACRL's new standards and "work to connect information literacy with the visual literacy initiatives" (Harris 2010, 523). Indeed, a
recent study by Brumberger at Virginia Tech, "Visual Literacy and the Digital
Native," concluded that Virginia Tech's students (often referred to as "digital natives" or "millennial learners") were "far from adept at producing and
interpreting visual communication" (Brumberger 2011, 44). Given this environment, faculty and librarians at colleges and universities are rethinking
their methodology as they develop new initiatives that incorporate visual
literacy standards into the curriculum.

Opportunity for Change

The ACRL (2011) asserts that "[t]he importance of images and visual media
in contemporary culture is changing what it means to be literate in the 21st
century." Based on this premise, it is imperative for universities and their
respective faculty members to provide the education and training needed
for our students to be competitive in a global economy. In order to reach
our goal of incorporating visual literacy standards at the University of Pittsburgh at Greensburg (Pennsylvania), we were excited to learn that the R. K.
Mellon Grant received by the Pitt-Greensburg campus specified an objective
of supporting faculty in curricular innovations incorporating digital, global,
interdisciplinary, and experiential elements. Such a goal cannot be easily
achieved without providing a critical campus component: a digital media lab.

Pitt-Greensburg is a regional campus offering baccalaureate degrees
grounded in traditional liberal arts disciplines to approximately 1,900 undergraduates. The Pitt-Greensburg campus places primary emphasis on teaching excellence while maintaining a commitment to scholarship and public
service. In 2011, Pitt-Greensburg applied for, and received, a 500,000-dollar
R. K. Mellon Grant to support faculty in curricular innovation incorporating
digital, global, interdisciplinary, and experiential elements. Consequently,
the Millstein Library at Pitt-Greensburg seized the opportunity to request
some funding for a digital media lab from the R. K. Mellon Grant that would
promote and enhance the curriculum in a secure yet collaborative location,
providing students and faculty in any discipline with the necessary tools to
work with digital media, including video, audio, imaging, and web publishing. Such a facility would allow users to develop their skills in visual literacy,

enabling "an individual to effectively find, interpret, evaluate, use, and create images and visual media" (ACRL 2011). Standard Six of the "ACRL Visual Literacy Competency Standards for Higher Education" specifically targets the design and creation of meaningful images and visual media by students: "The visually literate student uses a variety of tools and technologies to produce images and visual media" (ACRL 2011). Clearly, Pitt-Greensburg students would not be able to meet the ACRL visual literacy standards without the proper tools or equipment at their disposal.

A digital media lab located in the Millstein Library would not be without precedent. Many libraries have migrated to an information commons environment where students have access to equipment and space to experiment with image production tools and technologies and to develop proficiency in editing their multimedia projects. The Millstein Library already had a wireless network, group study rooms, comfortable seating areas for group project work, access to DirecTV, a mobile device lending program, and other amenities often associated with an information commons.

Planning for the Future

As the idea for a media lab in the library evolved, it was necessary to develop a coherent plan to request funding with all the key players on campus. A small working group was established and included the director of the library, the director of the computer center, the coordinator of the media and instructional technology services, the reference/instruction librarian, and two other technicians from the computer center and audiovisual services. Support and buy-in from these units was critical for the setup and ongoing maintenance for such a facility within the library. This group reached a consensus that this project was viable and would serve the needs of both students and faculty engaged in various projects across the curriculum that required a digital media component. It was agreed that the Millstein Library would provide a secure location on campus that would be available seven days a week during the fall and spring semesters. Another constraint in our plan was that we are a PC (personal computer) campus and could not offer Apple products in our facility.

As part of the planning process, we researched other digital media labs across the country and consulted with other librarians regarding the kind of equipment they had purchased and the pros/cons of different services they were offering on their campuses. In this regard, the Google spreadsheet titled "Multimedia Production Centers," produced by the Multimedia Production Discussion Group that is part of the American Library Association's Video Round Table, was extremely helpful (Video Round Table 2012). We also visited a new library information commons area to get a sense of what was working and what was not. This research, as well as the combined expertise of the working group, resulted in a list of items that we believed would meet the needs of our new media lab.

Securing Key Equipment

As part of our initial digital media lab at Millstein, we determined we would need a budget of approximately 20,000 dollars to begin this process and to offer the following services:

- Digital video/audio conversion from several formats to digital format
- Production of audio and video projects
- Scanning of large complex images and text for online portfolios or projects
- Large-format printing for presentations and conferences
- Color printing
- Music composition
- Lending of camcorders/digital cameras/audio recording devices and other pertinent equipment to Pitt-Greensburg students and faculty members

The funds we received and allocated were used for equipment, software, and port relocation. We did not purchase any additional furniture and instead repurposed tables and chairs already in the library. The equipment purchased for our new media lab to meet these services included:

- Two Dell OptiPlex 900 MiniTowers N-series with twenty-five-inch screens to accommodate audio and video projects

- Two licenses for Adobe Creative Suite 6 Master Collection (through the University of Pittsburgh) to download and edit videos for production
- Hewlett-Packard (HP) Color Laser Jet Enterprise printer for color printing
- HP DesignJet Z2100 forty-four-inch photo printer for color poster printing
- HP Scanjet to scan a variety of items in different formats
- Sony and Canon video cameras with tripods and digital cameras
- Audio and light equipment, including microphones and headphones compatible with both Sony and Canon devices
- Korg keyboard with Mixcraft and Sibelius software for both production of musical compositions as well as practice sessions for music students

Envisioning New Spaces

As with all new library services, space and budget constraints are critical. In our particular case, we seized an opportunity to apply for some grant money that had been received by the campus. We also had access to library endowment money that we combined with our proposal to make it more attractive to the administration. To obtain these funds and receive permission to use endowment money, we had to write an official proposal and have it approved by the campus administration.

Reallocation of space and furniture within the library was more problematic and required a plan of action. Once again, the working group we had established went into action and moved the project forward as a team. First, we addressed the library computer lab. Opened in 1995 with the new building, the enclosed computer lab room had been transformed over the years from a word-processing facility to a comfortable, if somewhat limited, lab with nine Dell devices and a large-capacity, black-and-white laser printer. These devices were heavily used by Pitt-Greensburg students all semester long. We had ten active hard-wired ports in this room and ample electrical power for additional devices. Approximately seventeen by twenty-four feet with a locked door, the computer lab had served us well over the years, but it did not allow for any collaborative space for students working jointly on projects and provided no flexibility. Consequently, we decided to reallocate some of the computer ports to a new open area in the library formerly occupied by empty microfilm cabinets and equipment. The new computer lab area had ample space for growth, multiple power plates, and the capacity to provide a more user-friendly area for students working on projects together. This first step, the reallocation of our computer lab, went smoothly during a quiet summer session.

The next step involved purchasing, setup, and secure housing of the equipment for the new digital media lab. Once the computer lab had been emptied and relocated, we allocated some locking cabinets that were not being used to hold the equipment that would circulate, such as the camcorders, tripods, and microphones. The university's computer center personnel assisted us in setting up our new high-end devices, keyboard, scanner, and printers and in troubleshooting new software. We were almost ready to introduce our new lab to the campus community, with one tiny exception: none of us knew how to use the new hardware or software.

Overcoming a Steep Learning Curve

In general, academic libraries have been at the forefront in developing new services to support student learning in collaboration with their respective faculties. "Multimedia expertise is becoming as commonplace for students as other areas of computer expertise and is being used in many career fields" (McCoy 2008, 158). Consequently, it is not surprising that librarians are once again delving into a new learning frontier with digital media labs. For our small library, the fall 2012 term was looming, and we could not afford to hire anyone to staff the facility, so it became incumbent on us to learn what we could in a relatively short period of time by picking the brain of our media services coordinator on how to use camcorders and edit movies; relying on the kindness of administrative assistants on the main Pitt campus who had vast experience in poster printing; purchasing books and completing tutorials on Adobe products; and having fun filming baby showers and summer trips with camcorders and then trying to edit our movies for

YouTube, adding images and sound with our new Creative Suite software package. Thankfully, the staff was on board and excited about this opportunity. After some significant "playtime" during the summer term, we felt more comfortable with the technology, had a better idea what to expect from this equipment and software, and felt confident that we could field most of the easier questions from students and faculty in the upcoming fall term. At this point, it became much easier to determine how to circulate the equipment through our library system, what new loan policies we might want to set up, and how we would market the facility to the campus community.

Marketing a Digital Media Lab

In many respects, it seems quite logical for public libraries to build and market new services such as a digital media lab. For example, deemed a Library as Incubator Project, the Carnegie Library of Pittsburgh launched a new program in 2012, The Labs @ CLP, where teen patrons can drop in or attend a workshop on learning about digital media and collaborate with specialists and mentors to help them with their projects (Dickerson 2013). Implementation of such a service at an academic library is a bit more complicated, but it can dovetail nicely with the library's mission "to provide and promote access to information resources...and to collaborate in the development of effective information, teaching, and learning systems" (University Library System 2014).

At Pitt-Greensburg, we marketed our new digital media lab through as many venues as we could manage. Our budget is limited, so we developed all our publicity in-house. Our first focus was the faculty, so we introduced our lab right before the start of the fall 2012 term, sending out e-mail and paper invitations to come to look at the space. Open informational sessions were held in the new lab to allow for questions, brainstorming, and hands-on training. Our focus was to convince faculty that they could integrate digital technology into the current curriculum and perhaps develop new courses that would utilize the lab. Brochures, postcards, and campus video screens in the student center were also used to publicize the lab to faculty and students, as was a "Digital Media Lab" LibGuide (Duck 2012). Approximately a dozen faculty members came to our sessions, while others corresponded with us via e-mail and telephone asking for more information.

If You Build It, They Will Come (Eventually)

Several years ago, a colleague at another academic institution remarked to me that "universities work glacially," alluding to the fact that sometimes it seems to take a millennium or two before you see any results related to your master plan, course revision, or new service. Libraries, while trying to be nimble in providing up-to-date services, are often confronted with this malaise within their own institution. We have to remind ourselves that collaboration with faculty colleagues takes time, effort, and constant care and feeding.

At Pitt-Greensburg, our new digital media lab has had some early successes. Feedback from both faculty and students has been very positive. During the fall 2012 semester, many freshman seminar classes required students to prepare a fifteen-minute video showcasing something (or someone) on the Greensburg campus. Circulation statistics from October through December 2012 indicated that fifty-four items (cameras, camcorders, tripods, etc.) had been checked out by students for this and other class assignments. Poster printing has proven to be very popular with students for class presentations, as we provide one free two-by-three-foot poster and twenty color copies per semester to each student. During the fall term, nineteen posters and 367 color prints were produced. Individual departments on campus have also requested posters, and they are happy to pay the reasonable fee of twenty-five dollars for larger items. Monies collected from this service are then funneled back into the supply budget for the lab. Video production, although not initially successful, is starting to catch on, and students are beginning to ask for other programs related to video production software and equipment items to complete their projects.

As our lab is more fully utilized, we anticipate that we will see higher circulation of equipment and more potential training sessions and projects with faculty members and classes. We have already been approached by a local videographer who has campus connections and is willing to work with us on developing some instructional efforts in this area. With continued support from key units on campus (the computer center, audiovisual services, and campus administration), possible expansion of the facility, and the introduction of new furnishings, the library will be well positioned to assist faculty to integrate the tools of the digital media lab into their curriculum.

As Deandra Little has suggested, "liberal education in the twenty first century needs to take seriously the visual as a fundamental way of knowing" (Little, Felten, and Berry 2010, 49). Hopefully, our new digital media lab will lead the way in helping our faculty develop new curriculum initiatives with the appropriate tools to foster important visual literacy skills for the twenty-first century.

REFERENCES

ACRL (Association of College and Research Libraries). 2011. "ACRL Visual Literacy Competency Standards for Higher Education." American Library Association. Approved October. www.ala.org/acrl/standards/visualliteracy.

Brumberger, Eva. 2011. "Visual Literacy and the Digital Native: An Examination of the Millennial Learner." *Journal of Visual Literacy* 30 (1): 19–47.

Dickerson, Molly. 2013. "The Labs @ Carnegie Library of Pittsburgh: Life After the Launch, Part One: Filmmaking at The Labs." The Library as Incubator Project. Posted January 25. www.libraryasincubatorproject.org/?p=8691.

Duck, Pat. 2012. "Digital Media Lab—Greensburg Campus." University of Pittsburgh. http://pitt.libguides.com/content.php?pid=363076 (redirects to updated site at http://pitt.libguides.com/c.php?g=12431).

Freeman, Geoffrey T. 2005. "The Library as Place: Changes in Learning Patterns, Collections, Technology, and Use." In *Library as Place: Rethinking Roles, Rethinking Space*, 1–9 Washington, DC: Council on Library and Information Resources.

Harris, Benjamin R. 2010. "Blurring Borders, Visualizing Connections: Aligning Information and Visual Literacy Learning Outcomes." *Reference Services Review* 38 (4): 523–35.

Little, Deandra, Peter Felten, and Chad Berry. 2010. "Liberal Education in a Visual World." *Liberal Education* 96: 44–49.

McCoy, Shelly. 2008. "Stirring the Pot: Combining Traditional and Innovative Services at the University of Delaware." *Microform and Imaging Review* 36 (4): 155–8. doi:10.1515/MFIR.2007.155.

University Library System. 2014. "Planning Documents." University of Pittsburgh. Accessed October 2. www.library.pitt.edu/planning-documents.

Video Round Table. 2012. "Multimedia Production Discussion Group." American Library Association. Last updated January 17. http://vrt.ala.org/wiki/index.php?title=Multimedia_Production_Discussion_Group.

PART V

INNOVATIVE SPACES

11

Participatory Spaces and Idea Box

Monica Harris

As libraries focus more on becoming true centers for creation and innovation, many librarians and administrators are stuck trying to determine how they will afford to buy media in all of the formats that their patrons want, employ degreed professionals at competitive salaries, and still find something in the budget to devote to a makerspace or digital media lab. Library professionals want the best for their patrons, and it is frustrating when the reality does not measure up to aspirations. Innovation is often born out of necessity due to very real constraints, and time and again, small nonprofit institutions have risen to that challenge. The Oak Park (Illinois) Public Library (OPPL) worked with exactly these kinds of limitations and created Idea Box, an immersive participatory community space that is constantly changing.

Idea Box is a nineteen-by-thirteen-foot space in the Main Library's vestibule. Formerly a privately owned café space, it has a large glass window and door that look into a simple room with drywall and a tile floor. The library uses this space to engage the community creatively, featuring an entirely new exhibit each month. Exhibits have offered a variety of experiences, but the focus of each is always on engaging every patron who walks through the door. Engagement usually centers around some kind of content creation, whether that means patrons taking a moment to add their thoughts or just to read those of their neighbors that have been displayed in the space. Each engagement is designed to last only a few minutes, giving every patron who walks through the door a few moments to surprise and delight them. It provides high value for the customers who visit every day, as there is always something new to look at or experience. For more casual users, the monthly changes inspire awe at how the library is always fresh and changing.

History

To explain a little more about how Idea Box began, let's start with a history of the space it is currently in. When the library lost its second coffee shop vendor in late 2010, library administration decided to take a moment to focus on whether they wanted to continue by searching out another tenant. Coffee is within easy walking distance at several local establishments, and there was support from the board that the library should find a way to use this high-value real estate in the library vestibule as a place to support the library mission. The Oak Park community also places a high value on art and culture, so Assistant Director Jim Madigan suggested that the space could serve as a secondary art gallery. Administration, under the leadership of then–Executive Director Dee Brennan, created a Customer Service Manager position whose responsibilities would include curating the new space.

Around the same time as the use of the café space was being shaped, OPPL had also been adding more focus to its programming plan and offerings. A new adult programming plan was revised in 2011 to include balance between several variables that would separate more traditional library programming from that which would attract new audiences and engage the community. Part of this balance was a specific focus on having more participatory programming, in which the audience contributes something to the experience of the program. In other words, a participatory program isn't one in which an expert releases knowledge to the audience; instead, the knowledge is shared among all of the participants.

The library still continued to host more traditional programming like author visits and book discussions, but it also offered more of a balance between those conventional programs and some new ideas. Soon it was hosting after-hours trivia events, speed dating, pie baking contests, and movieoke. As these new programs took shape, the community members who attended library programming changed as well. New audiences were being reached, and those new audiences were grateful for the connections they were making and sharing with the library and their greater community.

As the new Customer Service Manager for OPPL, I made the connection between what was already happening in terms of new programming and suggested that those same principles could be applied to a physical space in the library, namely, the Idea Box. The library had very loosely defined what Idea Box would offer; this was a way to bring focus to what we had created. We were heavily influenced by the work of museum innovator Nina Simon, whose blog *Museum 2.0* (http://museumtwo.blogspot.com) and 2010 book *The Participatory Museum* provided a great deal of the framework that we used to create the space. Her clear guidelines for the values of participation (including providing intrinsic value in the experience, creating quality outcomes, and providing constraints) allowed exhibit designers the opportunity to conceive creatively while providing a framework for success. She also provided methodology for evaluation that proved useful throughout that first year of the Idea Box.

Design Principles

After a short pop-up display of locally produced material from the Read/Write Library Chicago (formerly Chicago Underground Library) in March, the first exhibit under my direction and with a participatory focus began in April 2012. OPPL Assistant Manager of Children's Services Rory Parilac ran with an idea to create a poetry space by suggesting the library paint a large strip of magnetic paint around the perimeter of the space, stick up twenty sets of magnetic poetry, and just encourage the public to play. From the very beginning, Idea Box has been about encouraging collaboration between departments and sharing inspiration to create new things, so it's only appropriate that the first Idea Box exhibit was born this way. The only instructions to the public included the colorful bubble letters stuck up just outside the door: "April is National Poetry Month. Come in to Read or Write a Poem." The simplicity worked. Immediately, patrons wandered in to play with the available words to create their own poems, and some came in just to read the work of others.

This was the first opportunity we had to observe a phenomenon that has taken place over and over again in Idea Box. In his article "Participation Inequality: Encouraging More Users to Contribute," Jakob Nielsen (2006) highlighted the inequality between those who merely visit online communities and those who take the time to comment. He asserted that roughly 90 percent are lurkers, or those who read or observe activity without contributing. The remaining 10 percent are split between the 9 percent of users who contribute a little and the 1 percent of users who account for most of the contributions. What we found with this physical environment is that not everyone wanted to contribute thoughts or content, but many wanted to come in to read what their neighbors were writing.

Nielsen's (2006) suggestions for improving interactivity also informed the kinds of experiences we created. His first suggestion is also the one the exhibit design took most seriously: Make it easier to contribute. On the web, this might mean fewer barriers to entry like account registration or the absence of passwords or CAPTCHAs. In person, we determined this meant few directions to follow, simple processes, and very little invested time. With these limits in place, when informally surveyed, library customers reported viewing Idea Box as an added benefit to their daily library experience. They can choose to take a few minutes to contribute their thoughts or just to see what people in their community are up to. We've also designed the exhibits to appeal to patrons of all ages, providing a hands-on experience that can make anyone feel more creative and engaged.

Another prevailing principle that has emerged from the Idea Box is a commitment to its exhibits being both striking and ephemeral. One of the natural advantages to being in this space is that every patron who comes in and leaves the library must walk by Idea Box. The design of the glass windows looking into the shallow room also give it the feel of a showroom, a place that shows off what's new and interesting in the library and community. Taking note of this parallel, the Customer Service team started to look at the ways that retail establishments use their store windows effectively to bring customers inside, illuminate their brand, and encourage people to note that things are constantly changing. In particular, we looked at brands like Anthropologie, Paper Source, and large upscale department stores like Nordstrom and Macy's to see how they used their windows to attract customers. These diverse retail establishments are all committed to outlaying considerable effort to physical window displays in order to help define their brands and appeal to their demographics. We thought we could provide similar benefits by making sure that the Idea Box was visually striking and appealing and that exhibits looked different enough from one another that library users would be caught a little off guard by the change. The exhibits are constantly changing, which allows our public to be in a constant state of surprise and delight.

What is the simplest change you can make with the biggest impact? For OPPL, it has been paint. For less than two gallons of paint and a few hours of work from our facilities crew, the results are transformative at a very low price point. The Customer Service team has focused on finding connections with those on staff who have design or visual merchandising skills and has worked with them to help create the most attractive and interesting tableaus possible. By acknowledging that visual interest is important, we've been able to attract new talent and create exhibits that feel inviting and interesting.

Structure

At the time of this writing, Idea Box has been open one year, and in that time a successful structure has evolved to keep it running efficiently. Once the principles described earlier were successfully defined, the Customer Service department was able to take full ownership of the space. Responsibility moved away from one individual (in this case, the Customer Service Manager) to become a responsibility of the whole department. In doing so, a department made up of paraprofessional staff was able to stretch their own abilities and responsibilities to work on something creative and fulfilling as a part of the job. Library assistants also monitor the space, tidying and answering questions as they make their way into Idea Box several times an hour from the Welcome Desk.

While it was important that the Customer Service department have ultimate responsibility for the exhibits, it was also essential to have buy-in on the Idea Box from all over the organization in order to offer a strong explanation to a curious community. One way to do this was to allow anyone, from shelvers to administrators, to submit ideas in a shared spreadsheet. The Idea Box Think Tank is a committee featuring members from all over the organization, as well as a heavy representation of Customer Service stakeholders. They meet four times a year to discuss submissions and determine the quarterly schedule. Customer Service supervisors take turns accepting responsibility for each month's exhibit, building a team to ensure the implementation goes smoothly.

In 2013, Idea Box was given a budget line of 6,000 dollars to spend for the entire calendar year. This translates into roughly 300 to 500 dollars for each exhibit, leaving some money left over for evaluation tools that we hoped to purchase, such as a mounted door counter, and for additional equipment that could be helpful to future exhibits, like an iPad. Based on observation and representative samples, it is estimated that roughly 1,500 people a month enter Idea Box, with many others looking in from outside the glass walls.

Idea Box also took its first steps into social media in the spring of 2013, with a bracketed voting game, similar to March Madness, in the exhibit This or That Madness, which explored voting both in the physical space of Idea Box as well as through comments on the library's Facebook page. In-house voting far outweighed the results from online voting, but the comment voting associated with the exhibit created the largest engagement in the history of the library's social media presence. The Idea Box Think Tank hoped to find new ways to work with our Virtual Services department to improve relationships with the hyperlocal physicality of Idea Box.

Evaluation of participatory exhibits can be difficult, but Nina Simon (2010) offered some very good ideas in her book *The Participatory Museum*, including stating your goals for each exhibit and then looking back at each one to see if the behaviors and outcomes reflect those goals. She also noted that some good ideas ultimately don't work because there is not enough buy-in from staff, subject matter is not important enough to the user, or there is not enough of a development system to support the staff. One benefit of high community engagement with the Idea Box was that the community seemed much more apt than usual to share their opinions on the space. Staff members welcoming patrons coming into the library would often hear the most comments and questions about the Idea Box. They would write each comment down, and then all comments would be tabulated and analyzed at the end of the month by the Customer Service Manager. We were also able to view social media engagement with the Idea Box by searching for its mention on Twitter, Facebook, and Instagram, and seeing the photos and comments that the community posted. This kind of unfiltered reaction is valuable and allows the changing OPPL brand to be viewed by those outside its normal sphere of influence. When the Idea Box Think Tank met quarterly, there was always a discussion of the previous quarter's exhibits so that we could gauge staff interest and perceived success, and these were further considered when deciding selections for the upcoming quarter. As of this writing, an Idea Box exhibit has never been repeated.

Example Exhibits

Best Books (August 2012)

Best Books is a simple and interactive display that encourages visitors to take a moment to write (or draw!) about a book they love on a Post-it note and hang it on the wall. This exhibit was inspired in part by the sticky note wall at the Smithsonian's traveling exhibit *Suited for Space*, which encouraged participants to share their drawings of astronauts and space travel. Among the simplest exhibits designed for Idea Box, this one featured blank white walls and a single desk along with these simple instructions: *Share your favorite books with us. Choose a sticky note. Write (or draw or scribble) about a book. Stick it up!* These simple but open-ended instructions encouraged user creativity that we hadn't seen until this point. User-directed cues started to appear early in the process, including directions on one Post-it for people to put checkmarks on the books they like. Commentary on other books started to appear as well, with some people agreeing on a favorite and others helping remember the name of an author. Thousands of Post-its were shared over the month and started to appear on the glass in the front of Idea Box, on the floor, and on the ceiling. The open-ended instructions encouraged a playful attitude that manifested itself in totally new ways.

Contribute Your Creativity to a Tee (December 2012)

In an effort to collaborate with the community while still staying within the space's defined participatory principles, OPPL took the opportunity to partner with another organization for December's exhibit. We worked with Lindsay Harmon, librarian for the American Academy of Art in Chicago, to offer an undergraduate student contest that would allow students to compete for a spot in the Idea Box in exchange for 500 dollars for materials and an opening. Ten separate student projects were proposed, and we chose Contribute Your Creativity to a Tee by artist Danny Murphy. Murphy created a giant four-by-eleven-foot pegboard, drilled additional holes for a higher resolution, and then hand-painted 10,000 golf tees in six rainbow colors. The result was a giant image board for making pixel art, reminiscent of a giant Lite-Brite. It was a wonderful way to engage the public with using more art and design in a familiar way.

Park It (February 2013)

One of the most successful exhibits to come out of the Idea Box Think Tank was Park It, which created a summery park in the frigid Chicago February. Customer Service Supervisors Kelly Knowles and Julie Meo conceived and implemented a full park, featuring park benches, a cloudy blue sky, Astroturf, the sounds of birds singing, and a real working fountain. New outdoor equipment like rubber balls, jump ropes, and Frisbees appeared in the space each day, encouraging visitors to play in as well as just experience the park. Children immediately ran inside to play, and users of all ages sat on the benches to chat with one another or stopped to read for a bit. The whimsy of the space and the unexpectedness of seeing such a summery space just a few feet away from the snow outside brought huge smiles to customers all month long.

The Future

Idea Box is just one step in a future that engages with the community in an active way. The OPPL's Main Library lobby is looking forward to a renovation that will create a large, open lounge space that can accommodate pop-up musical and dance performances or small-scale creation classes. We also expect the renovation to allow for experiences that will be much easier to accommodate in this more malleable space. The Idea Box Think Tank team members also dream of creating a portable Idea Box that can easily travel outside of Idea Box's four walls to community festivals, parades, or anywhere that community members are getting together.

Exploring how creativity and creation can enliven a community is an interesting pursuit, and, as yet, the Idea Box Think Tank team cannot provide any concrete answers about how this project is changing the community. What we can measure is just how much our visitors have embraced it. Every month we receive dozens of unsolicited comments about how much people are enjoying Idea Box. They are sometimes sad to see an exhibit go, but they are always excited to wait to see what is coming next.

REFERENCES

Nielsen, Jakob. 2006. "Participation Inequality: Encouraging More Users to Contribute." Nielsen Norman Group. Posted October 9. www.nngroup.com/articles/participation-inequality.

Simon, Nina. 2010. *The Participatory Museum*. Santa Cruz, CA: Museum 2.0.

12

"Like a Kid in a Candy Store"

Marketplaces in Public Libraries

Daisy Porter-Reynolds

In libraries, we often hear references to "the retail model" or "merchandising your products." Why would a library—a public, tax-supported, nonprofit institution—want to adopt a model like this? After all, libraries aren't in it for the money. While libraries are not trying to maximize profits like retail stores, it is important to remember what we are trying to do. Most library professionals would say that at least part of their mission includes putting books in the hands of readers, and this goal is where the Marketplace comes in.

The library Marketplace concept was pioneered at San José (California) Public Library (SJPL) in the late 1990s by Branch Manager Ruth Barefoot, who once worked for a bookstore. She began shelving popular books and movies face out near the library's entrance so that every customer entering the library would walk past them and have the opportunity to browse. Later, SJPL made this a service standard across all locations. At one of the SJPL branches that I managed, the traffic flow was designed so that customers had to walk through the Marketplace in order to get to any other destination in the library. Many of them stopped to browse before moving along. The book and DVD covers did all the selling, which is exactly what publishers and studios intended them to do. There isn't a need for libraries to reinvent the marketing wheel because publishers have already spent big bucks on cover design to drive up sales.

SJPL's version of the Marketplace involves pulling out specific collections from the stacks, such as Home and Garden, Careers, and Computers, and putting every item into the Marketplace alongside the DVDs, CDs, and new books. Depending on the branch's community needs, other collections might be highlighted in the Marketplace, such as fotonovelas or Vietnamese movies. New books are periodically moved to the stacks to make room for more, but the Careers and other Marketplace collections remain there permanently. Customer feedback, both anecdotal and statistical, has been overwhelmingly positive; circulation tripled over the initial fourteen years of Marketplace implementation, from 4.8 million in 1994–1995 to 14.9 million in 2009–2010.

At Arlington Heights (Illinois) Memorial Library (AHML), we rolled out a Marketplace of our own in January 2013, to great applause from a community that expects the best. The title of this chapter, "Like a Kid in a Candy Store," comes from my favorite customer comment card, one we received the day after the Marketplace opened. My second-favorite comment? "Been coming [to AHML] since 1984 and this is worth the wait."

Why We Did This

The Marketplace was implemented as part of AHML's new service model, along with a staffing reorganization and a building renovation. Redesigning the library to match the way our customers use it, we combined service points, added conference rooms and a tech training center, built our first teen room, and created a relaxing reading area with armchairs in front of a fireplace. To continue to support our emphasis on popular materials, we created the Marketplace.

We believed that the adult stacks were not as customer-friendly as library offerings should be; the materials were shelved spine out and organized, as at most libraries, by Dewey Decimal Classification for nonfiction and alphabetically by author for fiction. Rather than sending off customers to peer at spine labels for nonintuitive codes like 641.563 written in twelve-point font, we wanted to direct them to a shelf marked Cookbooks. We also planned to offer multiple copies of new and popular titles in order to reduce wait times; at the same time, we wanted a true browsing collection without holds lists, so that a customer could pop in and find a best seller right there on the shelf just waiting for him or her to take it home. Finally, we intended to make browsing more appealing by shelving each book face out so as not to hide its own built-in advertising—the cover.

Categories, Not Dewey

Unlike at SJPL, we wanted AHML's Marketplace focus to be on new and popular materials, not specific categories that would live there permanently. Our selectors wanted to be sure to choose the right categories for the Marketplace so that customers would find what they were looking for as easily and quickly as possible. Categories should be neither too narrow (Cozy Mysteries would look sparse) nor too broad (customers might not think to look under Home Economics for cookbooks). The selectors consulted with our Information Services team to learn what customers asked for most often. Our master list now includes five fiction categories, such as Suspense and Mystery, and sixteen nonfiction categories, such as Biographies, Sports, Pop Culture, and Travel. The Marketplace also offers new DVDs and Blu-Rays, new CDs, and video games. About 18,000 items are shelved there at any given time.

The highlight of our Marketplace, though, is the Trending category. This is the first collection that customers see when they enter the Marketplace, and it changes every few days based on what's happening in the news and in popular culture. In the early months of 2013, we featured books about the papal conclave; several copies of *The Hobbit* during the week the movie was released; the latest issue of *People* magazine; a history of the Second Amendment; and much more. Our selectors have already made sure that we purchase a balanced collection of books on controversial topics like gun control, and the customer services advisors who choose what to put in Trending use the same care when stocking the shelves. In order to make the process of transferring items in and out of Trending as quick and easy as possible, we alter the book's item status in our integrated library system, in lieu of changing the item's location code. This way, the work can be done by the customer services advisors rather than traveling back to the catalogers. Even better, after a customer checks out an item, its Trending status is removed when we check it back in, with no additional work for staff.

Ordering, Cataloging, and Processing

Staff in AHML's Collection Services Group catalog and process each book individually upon its arrival at the library. However, for the Marketplace opening-day collection, we contracted with Baker & Taylor for shelf-ready materials and arranged for them all to be delivered the week before the Marketplace was set to open.

We wanted to reduce the number of labels and stickers we placed on these books—and on the collection as a whole—so we could offer a clean, streamlined look. It was also important to be efficient in terms of staff processing time while also keeping our shelf-ready cost per item to a minimum. Therefore, we don't put any "new" tape, genre stickers, or even call numbers on most of the Marketplace materials. Fiction and nonfiction categories alike receive labels with the category name on them and the date of acquisition—that's it. Only our "general nonfiction" category has a Dewey number on the spine. If an item is eventually reshelved in the stacks, staff will process it again with the appropriate call number and other labeling, as necessary.

The Marketplace is a priority for shelvers, to be completed before shelving of any other collection. To easily identify which books, movies, and music were Marketplace bound, we asked Baker & Taylor to cover each spine label with a brightly colored overlay. Initially, we had thought all overlays would be the same color, but after consulting with our Customer Services staff, we realized that customers wanted to be able to tell the difference between a book that was holdable (meaning they might not be able to renew it because a hold might be placed on it after checkout) and those that were not holdable and thus always renewable at least once. We decided on two different-colored overlays, yellow (holdable) and blue (renewable), for this reason. This also made it easier for staff pulling books for the holds list to determine which copies could fulfill a hold and which could not.

Shelving and Merchandising

The purpose of the Marketplace is browsing and discovery. We want our customers to spot it from across the room, eyes drawn to the colors and symmetry, and wander over to check it out. We envision that, once there, the customer may begin with the DVDs, for example, but end up drawn to a book across the aisle due to its appealing cover or title. The aesthetics of this area really matter. This is why we've trained our shelvers to merchandise, not shelve, in the Marketplace.

Simply put, merchandising is displaying library materials in an attractive way that will encourage customers to pick them up and, potentially, check them out. The principles of library merchandising include:

- Most, if not all, of the collection is displayed face out to allow the publisher's or studio's marketing—the covers—to sell the items.

- Larger items go on the bottom and middle, smaller ones on the top and sides. This creates a pleasant symmetry that catches customers' eyes from across the room.

- Like colors or images are placed next to each other for more visual appeal.

- Items are placed completely face out, not fanned or stacked. Customers are less likely to take items that look like they're there for display rather than for use.

- Multiple copies are displayed together. As with the previous principle, this encourages customers to pick up an item from a display, in this case without feeling like they're taking the last copy. The term we used at SJPL was *a feeling of plenty*.

Shelving is easier with this model! Our shelvers don't need to put everything in precise order; indeed, they can't since the books don't have Dewey numbers. I have encouraged them to be creative with their "shelve like items together" freedom, such as putting all of the books with a shoe or a face on the cover together or grouping all of the green books. In the time that the Marketplace has been open, I haven't seen much of this yet. I hope that the shelvers grow more comfortable doing this as time passes.

While shelving is easier, pulling holds is harder. The reserves staff spend more time working on the pull list than they used to because the items aren't in strict order. It helps that, shortly before we created the Marketplace, we changed the pull list structure so that any item attached to a bibliographic record could fill the hold. Reserves staff also know that they can ignore any item with a blue spine overlay because those items do not fill holds.

What's Not in the Marketplace

We never intended for AHML to be Dewey number–free. Dewey numbers play an important role in the stacks, where the best tools for customers and staff to find books are a robust catalog and a strict shelf order. Similarly, when looking for an author's backlist, it's helpful for all of the books by that author to be shelved together by last name. We continue to shelve this way outside of the Marketplace.

About 9 percent of the library's adult collection is in the Marketplace, which means 91 percent is not. Right now, almost every newly acquired adult book, movie, video game, and CD is shelved there, but not quite all. While our basic computing books live in the Marketplace, coding and other technical manuals live in the stacks. Business books go in the stacks, as do more academic books that would not find a bigger audience even when merchandised.

Our large-print and audiobook collections also reside outside the Marketplace, even though they're of general popular interest. Our customer services advisors recommended we keep these two collections separate. Customers seeking audiobooks and large-print books tend to be format-driven rather than content-driven. In other words, the format is a more important consideration than the newness of the content. So that these customers wouldn't have to browse in two different locations, we shelved all audiobooks together and all large-print books together, outside the Marketplace.

Customer Reaction

Simply put, customers love the Marketplace. Most of the customer comments that rise to the administrative level are complaints. Not so in the early days of the Marketplace. My inboxes, physical and virtual, have been filled with customer compliments about how easy it is for them to find items, how much they enjoy the look and feel of the space, and, my favorite, how they are checking out more items than usual because the covers are so alluring.

Aside from anecdotes, the statistics from the Marketplace's first six weeks demonstrate just how popular it is. For example, 43 percent of the collection is checked out on any given day, compared with 23 percent for the library as a whole. Even when comparing Marketplace circulation to our former New Books collection—its closest equivalent—these items are going out much more often. To me, the stats are even more important than the compliments because most customers will never fill out a comment card. The primary way that customers speak to us is via their actions, such as placing holds, reserving computers, attending programs, or checking out materials.

A few customers, of course, are not as happy with the Marketplace as the rest. This is a normal, expected part of institutional change. One man wrote on a comment card, "Not having a [Dewey] number on those books is crazy!" He didn't explain why, so I wasn't able to address his concern. Another customer felt it was too loud in the area for her to sit and read. Aside from these two, the only negative reactions I've had were from guest borrowers who are not residents of our town. They were disappointed that they weren't eligible to check out materials from this developing collection.

What We Learned

As of October 2013, we've had eight months of Marketplace feedback and statistics. These numbers continue to support the concept. For example, the Marketplace collection represents 7.5 percent of the adult collection, yet is responsible for 25 percent of adult circulation. These high statistics are not simply due to the newness of the items. Marketplace circulation is 20 percent higher than that for our previous New Books and New Movies sections from before we began.

We have also learned that it took a couple of extra steps to help our customers feel comfortable in the Marketplace. For example, the signage we installed isn't quite enough to help them find what they need in the largest sections, Fiction and General Nonfiction. Finding the beginning of the alphabet or of Dewey numbering is not as intuitive as we'd hoped, so we will add numbers and letters to our category signs. We will also be adding fiction authors' names to the spines of books; we had thought that since the books were not shelved spine out, this wouldn't be necessary, but it turned out that both staff and customers missed the consistent placing and font of the author names when searching. We will continue to find ways to make the collection easier to navigate and use.

What's Next

Libraries across the country are in constant flux as they try to predict what customers will want next from their libraries. The key to changing a library service is to stay flexible and keep tweaking along the way. In the future, we will continually revisit the book categories to make sure we picked the right ones and add new ones as needed. We are installing an e-book discovery station in the area so that customers can browse our virtual collections. In our Children's Department, we're piloting what we call the Mini-Mart, a kid version of the Marketplace that opened in summer 2014. We don't want to leave out the teens, of course, so we also added a teen version later in 2014.

As more and more bookstores close, and as e-books and streaming video become more popular purchases, libraries may be the primary place for people to browse print books. It's up to us to make the experience intuitive, fun, and valuable.

PART VI

INNOVATIVE PROGRAMS

13

Apprentices of the Book Empire at a Glance

Amy Holcomb and Anna Fillmore

The Apprentices of the Book Empire (ABE) program facilitates a creative learning experience for elementary-school-aged children. It modernizes a typically traditional type of library program—a writing club—by including a twist. In this incarnation, we mimic the publishing industry, with the library as the publisher and the librarians running the program representing the publisher. The kids are the apprentices, and they are the authors of their own stories and the illustrators of others' stories. The apprentices have no say in who their illustrator is, who they are assigned to as an illustrator, or what their final product looks like. "Published" stories are cataloged and circulate for one year. Youth Services retains previous years' works for an unset time frame.

In developing this program, librarians brainstormed program titles. In that process, Apprentices of the Book Empire became a placeholder name as other titles were considered. However, ABE has a nice ring to it and conveniently defines the purpose of the program. Using the term *apprentices* implies learning a trade or skill, and that's exactly what ABE strives to do within the context of creating a book.

Goals

The main goal of ABE is to allow an opportunity for children to use the library as a place to engage in creative collaboration. Writing clubs and programs have been incorporated in youth services for some time, but ABE takes participants beyond the writing experience and into the publishing world. Because the program requires children to arrive with a finished story, it centers on discussion, experimentation, and collaboration in illustrating and publishing rather than on the process of writing. This makes the program unique to the library and sets a different tone from that of a school assignment.

Planning

We weighed the timing requirements of other programs, holidays, and the time commitment of all participants, including staff, in determining the best time of year and the scope for ABE. After weighing in all the factors, ABE became a weekly, one-hour program that meets for five weeks and is open to children in grades two through six. Our department strives to provide programming opportunities for children from birth through high school, and programming for elementary-school-aged children is often inconsistent in its offerings. ABE fills this gap and offers an opportunity outside the norm of library programs and classes. The five-week time frame gives sufficient time to the apprentices to illustrate their assigned stories and gives the librarians enough time to cover key components related to the illustrating and publishing processes. The number of participants is set at a minimum of eight and a maximum of twelve.

Publicity

Getting the word out is a creative process in its own right. The Northbrook (Illinois) Public Library's community tends to be well educated, and parents often look for educational programs or classes in Youth Services. ABE presents itself as not only education but also an opportunity for children to showcase their work so it appeals to both the parent and the child. ABE utilizes traditional resources like the library's website, bimonthly newsletter, and biweekly e-mail blasts. However, ABE is a unique, almost niche program that requires extra effort to recruit attendees. Librarians extend publicity efforts through social media, hoping to attract parents who determine ABE is a great fit and creative outlet for their children. After the first year, testimonies from previous participants and word-of-mouth recommendations from their parents help to fill registration rather quickly.

Cross-Departmental Collaboration

The success of ABE largely depends on establishing collaboration between the Circulation and Technical Services departments with Youth Services programming staff before the program begins. Since the ultimate goal of the program is publication of a book, Technical Services is consulted during the planning stages of the program in order to determine basic criteria for item records. Fortunately, Northbrook Public Library has an enthusiastic and creative team of catalogers who immediately supported the program. Working with the established record criteria, the catalogers assign the ABE items a specific call number (JUV APPRENTICE), item number, and home location. Genre form is Short stories and Northbrook (Ill.) | xAuthors (local author) is added in the 691 MARC field.

Circulation consults once a sample book is available and when the designated shelving space is determined. Since the ABE collection is essentially a boutique collection and each year's books circulate for one year, temporary shelving above a picture book range is the best location for staff and the public. This location is highly visible to patrons and is near the Youth Services Desk. The ABE books closely resemble the picture book collection, and with maximum exposure, the collection hopefully inspires homegrown writing and illustrating.

The librarians request that the Circulation Manager weigh in on the checkout period and possible fines. Since the items would be shelved near the picture books, it makes the most sense to allow the same checkout period of three weeks for the ABE items. No fines or damage fees are assigned to the items. In the event that an ABE book is damaged or goes missing, a color copy can be easily made from the original copies given to participants (see later for more on this). As of this writing, no items have been lost or damaged.

Supplies and Resources

As with most programs, ABE has to be completed on a budget. Following the general program budget guideline of the Youth Services department, ABE is allotted thirty dollars for its duration. To maximize the usage of funds, the program uses readily available supplies from the Youth Services department, like coloring utensils and specialty paper, as well as from the Business Office, like sheet protectors and name tags. The only supplies requiring purchase are three-ring binders, which hold the final ABE works. In ABE's pilot year, the largest, most unexpected expense was the book release celebration, which could have been managed with more fiscal responsibility. Luckily, enough funds were available, and, thankfully, that mistake has not been repeated.

In addition, it is important that ABE uses resources specific and unique to the library. The most important resource used at every session is the one that is bountiful in libraries—books—and lots of them. The apprentices are exposed to different types of illustrated children's books at each session, including picture books, graphic novels, illustrated chapter books, and novels.

The Timeline

Over five weeks, the apprentices participate in a miniworkshop on a specific topic. The workshops are designed to develop the participants' awareness of the types of illustrations and how those types of illustrations are used to tell stories. For example, ABE includes an exercise using *Zin! Zin! Zin! A Violin* by Lloyd Moss to show how a story can be told within a larger story using illustrations. In this case, Moss includes a storyline following two cats and a mouse within the overarching story of the orchestra. Limited discussion about the publication process is also included, namely, how authors are subject to relinquishing control of the artwork for and even the titles of their works.

Over the five weeks, apprentices are expected to create at least three illustrations for their assigned stories. The librarians set the illustration due date for one week after the last meeting. Working with that deadline, a publication date is set for two weeks after, which guarantees completion of the books and keeps the librarians on task.

The final step of the preparation process is collecting as many of the stories as possible before the first session. A few of the participants hand theirs in at the beginning of the first session. This gives the librarians a little more time to enter the stories into a Word document if they were handwritten. Having the stories done before the program started is an important part of ABE: other than some editing, library staff members are not involved in the writing process.

In the Workroom

Session 1

In the first session, two librarians who co-present the program start by greeting the program participants at the door, giving them their apprentice name tags, and playing an icebreaker game. One fun idea for an icebreaker game is to tape a picture or name of a popular book character like Harry Potter to the back of each participant and give the group four minutes to ask yes-or-no questions to figure out who they are. Following the icebreaker, the librarians, transformed into publishing moguls, give a brief overview of the program. The apprentices are informed that they will receive their illustration assignments the following week. This allows the librarians time to enter the remaining stories into a Word document and to make appropriate pairings. The apprentices are eager to find out with whom they will exchange books, and when they do discover their partners, they quickly get to work pitching their ideas. ABE exemplifies the good nature of children and their willingness to work together regardless of one another's ages or stories. It is incredible to witness.

For the first miniworkshop, the librarians load the table with a rich assortment of picture and chapter books, particularly those with which the participants are unlikely to be familiar. The ABE participants are instructed to find, without opening any books, a funny book. The children take turns dissecting the cover of the book they picked to the rest of the group and explain why they could tell that it was a funny book even though they had never heard of it or hadn't even looked at a single page. The participants are all able to do this in their own words with very little prompting. Some of the details they noticed were that funny books often:

- use bright and light colors,
- feature a cartoon type of drawing,
- use an informal font for the title, and
- use a lot of white space.

They also noticed that although sometimes the words of the title indicated to the reader that the book was a funny book, this could be done entirely through visual cues. In fact, it was possible to take a serious sounding title and still make the cover "read" as humorous through visual features.

The same exercise is repeated, with the participants finding serious books, fantasy books, and so forth, based solely on the covers. If too many participants present on the same type of book, the pacing becomes too slow. This is easily corrected by having five to six participants looking for and presenting on each type. The participants are encouraged to compare their observations with the observations of others from other types of books. From this exercise, the participants noted that illustrations carry a lot of information—in fact, they carry as much information as text does. They concluded that illustrations are excellent at conveying the tone or mood of the story.

A follow-up exercise to figuring out how a story is expressed through the visual presentation of a book is finding books with specific mediums like photographs, collage, line drawings, and watercolors. Librarians lead a discussion, asking if certain illustration mediums lend themselves to specific genres or moods. They then introduce the concept of white space and direct participants to race to find five examples of dominant use of white space. After the participants find five examples, librarians lead a group discussion on the white space and what it conveys within the selected books.

The primary activity of identifying the mood of a book by its cover is followed by the participants reading out loud several stories that their peer participants had written. The first session concludes with a "Thought Assignment" that is sent home with them:

Think about the type of story you wrote. What's the genre? Mood? Length? How do these factors influence the type of illustrations you'd like to see in your story? Come back next week with an idea of what the illustrations, including the cover, should look like for your story. You will share this with your assigned illustrator.

Session 2

The miniworkshop of this second session is "unillustrating" a picture book using *Olivia* by Ian Falconer, a book with which many children are familiar. When the text of this popular thirty-two-page book is typed into a Word document by library staff, it is three-quarters of one page long. This is very surprising to the ABE participants. The text is read aloud by a librarian without the illustrations and then read aloud again with the illustrations. This provides much fodder for discussion about the decisions in pacing, page turns, text placement, and choice of illustration in order to best tell the story. Listening to a story first followed by listening and looking at the illustrations effectively demonstrates how illustrations can both support and extend the story that the text tells. The publishing norm of stories being submitted without illustrations and another person doing the illustrations is introduced. As previously stated, it is ABE's goal to mimic this process, and the participants discuss this characteristic of picture book publishing.

This brings the program to a very dramatic moment: the illustrator assignments. The librarians pair participants based on age, length of stories, and genre of stories. Having participants close in age or in the same grade work together can result in better complementing illustrations of the individual works. Participants with longer stories are also paired together and face a bigger challenge of illustration selection and placement. The pairings are unveiled using envelopes with the participants' names, and immediately after, illustrators and authors meet and discuss their stories. This is the chance for the authors to share their vision for how the illustrations should look. We caution the authors that the illustrators could choose to disregard author suggestions. Copies of the stories are handed out so each illustrator has a week to read the story and begin thinking about how to approach the illustrations.

The session concludes, again, with different participants reading several of the original ABE stories out loud.

Session 3

In the third session, ABE examines how illustrations can tell a parallel story not mentioned in the text, and how illustrations can foreshadow plot developments. Librarians and apprentices look for and find examples of these in books selected for this purpose and discuss these examples. *Officer Buckle and Gloria* by Peggy Rathman provides a good example of illustrations telling a parallel story that augments the text when Gloria can be seen amusing the crowd with her tricks while Officer Buckle lectures. In *Zin! Zin! Zin! A Violin*, a cat-and-mouse chase takes place during the entire book but is never mentioned in the text.

Books with good examples of the illustration providing plot foreshadowing are *Oh, No!* by Candace Fleming and Eric Rohmann, *Chickens to the Rescue* by John Himmelman, and *Jeremy Draws a Monster* by Peter McCarty. In *Oh, No!*, tiny glimpses of the tiger can be spied here and there as the animals fall into the pit one by one, well before the text mentions the big cat. In *Chickens to the Rescue*, a chicken can be seen witnessing every disaster scene prior to the rescue, except for the last disaster when no rescue occurs. The visual foreshadowing occurs in *Jeremy Draws a Monster* when early in the book the text states, "He never went outside" and Jeremy is seen gazing out the window at a group of six kids playing ball. Those same six kids show up again at the very end of the book, asking Jeremy, "Do you want to play ball?"

ABE also looks at full-spread illustrations versus smaller graphics and what effect this choice has on pacing.

Apprentices are then instructed to determine the number of illustrations they think they need (with a minimum of four) and where in the story the illustrations should go. The rest of the time they devote to this.

The session concludes with a librarian reading an original ABE story out loud.

Session 4

The fourth session is primarily a work session. The apprentices meet in the interactive computer lab and design their covers and title pages. Librarians provide sample templates for the covers and title pages for the apprentices to start from, but final design choices are their own. The apprentices then move back into the activity room and work on their illustrations.

Session 5

About half of the apprentices finish their illustrations in this final session and hand them in, while the rest take them home and work one more week on them. Parents or guardians fill out a catalog authorization contract so their children's names can appear in our online public catalog (see the next section for more on this).

Putting It All Together

Initially, the books were imagined as bound, laminated pages, something that could be finalized at Kinkos and not take up much space. However, as the apprentices worked on their illustrations, we quickly discovered that the initial bound item we had envisioned would not do. First was the issue of using the illustrations effectively. Most did not fit in a nice spot on a page of text but required the text to work around the illustrations. Second was an issue with shelving. The books needed to be more book-like, with a spine for cataloging and front and back covers for durability and standing. We decided to use black, one-inch, three-ring "view" binders with front and back cover sleeves as well as a spine insert. The book pages would be contained in plastic sheet protectors secured on the binder rings.

Constructing the book pages was fairly time intensive. The two co-presenting librarians selected six titles each to construct. For each book, illustrations are selected from the works of the apprentice. Then, the librarians physically cut and paste text to accompany the selected illustrations, using card stock as the backing page and other textured or colored papers for design accents. Pages are numbered by hand in the lower right corner. Take-home copies for the apprentices are made by hand as well, using a color photocopier, and result in double-sided, laminated pages held together by white plastic, slide-on spines.

The illustrators are responsible for creating covers and title pages for their assigned stories. During construction, two pages are added by the librarians: a teaser or summary page for the back cover written by the librarian who constructed the book and a final page of the book that briefly explains what the ABE program is and lists all the stories by title, author, and illustrator.

Apprentices of the
Book Empire Author Contract

Northbrook Public Library requests permission to publish, for circulation, the stories written and illustrated by your minor child

_____.

(Child's name)

The child will receive one copy of the story he/she has written and one copy of the story he/she has illustrated.

In addition, these stories from the Apprentices of the Book Empire program will circulate for one year. Circulation will begin on November 2, 2012, and end on November 1, 2013. The circulating copies of the stories will remain in possession of the Library and will reside in the Youth Services Office.

For circulation, the stories will be entered into the Library's searchable catalog. Each story will have a unique library record, accessible during the circulation time period of one year.

The Library will include the following information in the stories' searchable records as part of the publication process:

- Child's name—author
- Child's name—illustrator
- Story title
- Date of publication

If you prefer to have your child's first name and last initial listed, please indicate above.

(continued on next page)

FIGURE 13.1
Apprentices of the Book Empire Author Contract

The Author Contract

Apprentices are required to have a contract signed by a parent or guardian in order to have their names, either first and last or first and last initial, listed in the item record for the catalog (see figure 13.1). The contract lists the personal information that would be used in the item record as well as the

(continued from previous page)

Signature of this permission slip hereby gives consent to North-brook Public Library to publish stories written and illustrated by the minor listed above, following the outlined criteria necessary to do so.

Parent/Guardian Name: _____

Parent/Guardian Signature: _____

Date: _____

Thank you for your child's participation in the Apprentices of the Book Empire program.

Northbrook Public Library—Youth Services
1201 Cedar Lane, Northbrook, IL 60062
847.272.4300

dates of circulation and the storage location of the item after the circulation period. Contracts are required to be returned by the illustration deadline, which is one week after the last session. Librarians provide copies of the signed contracts for the parents/guardians. The library copies remain on file in the Youth Services Office.

Cataloging and Shelving

Since Youth Services staff consulted with the Technical Services department about this program at its inception, the cataloging process is seamless. As each book is completed, Technical Services catalogs and processes the item. Records are double cross-checked to confirm names and titles. A local author sticker is added to the inside front cover, and the bar code is placed on the title page. And once the collection is cataloged, Circulation staff are notified and reminded of the shelving location.

Celebrate Good Times

With the books finished, bound, and cataloged, it's time to celebrate and share. ABE plans a Book Release Celebration and distributes invitations to the apprentices and their families, and to the staff at the library. At the celebration, the books are available to read and check out. This is the first time the apprentices get to see the finished products, and they are very excited. They sign the circulating copies of the books, and each participant receives a laminated copy of both the book he or she authored and the one he or she illustrated. The highlight, however, might be looking up their names on the library catalog that we have available on a laptop and a few iPads. The apprentices line up to do this as they drink their cider and eat their apple slices.

The local paper is contacted for the celebration, and a reporter attends to take pictures and conduct interviews, which is great publicity for the library. After the celebration, a brief article about ABE and the books it creates is posted on the homepage of the library website as well as on social networks like Facebook and Tumblr. A tabletop sign advertising the books is placed next to the shelving unit where the books are filed.

Let's Do It Again

From the first two sessions of the program, the librarians' evaluations are more than acceptable. ABE had great participation, with twelve attendees in its pilot run and ten in its second year. Considering the time commitment and work required by participants, ten and twelve are big numbers. And ABE had almost 100 percent attendance for all sessions, which says a lot about the participants' interest in the program. In addition, both sessions of the program had many interested patrons who were turned away. Feedback from both the apprentices and their families is overwhelmingly positive, including such observations that a child who often writes but is never able to finish a story was motivated to bring his or her writing full circle. As of this writing, we have yet to receive any negative comments.

In future sessions, the librarians plan on building in one-on-one editing sessions with each apprentice in the beginning of the program. Past sessions had some writing issues that did not get as much attention as they deserved. In addition, future ABE programs will include more structured in-program time to do the illustrations. Having the apprentices storyboard the story before they begin drawing is also a possibility.

Two staff members will continue to co-present the program. In ABE's pilot session, librarians spent two to three hours constructing each book, partly because it had never been done before and partly because the librarians really wanted to present a high-quality product. In the second year, librarians allotted less time to the book construction, using simplified designs and more readily available page templates from Microsoft Publisher. The actual time spent planning for the program is minimal, especially now that the foundation exists and we have a better understanding of what to expect from participants.

Another likely change will be to decrease the amount of time spent reading the original stories aloud. Although very enjoyable, it takes up a lot of time. Reading the entire story can be replaced with reading several paragraphs. This will free up more time for discussion and illustration work.

Facilitating the creation of original content by kids and creating the opportunity for kids to collaborate on creative projects is a very worthwhile and enjoyable project, and one that is central to many libraries' missions. Expanding upon ABE and creating similar programs for older kids is a goal our librarians plan on implementing. This program will focus on graphic novels but again be centered around creative collaboration, enabling the creation of original content and providing a platform for sharing the results.

14

Monsters, Rockets, and Baby Racers

Stepping into the Story with Children and Young People

Matt Finch and Tracie Mauro

ibrary activities for children and young people don't have to cost the earth—and as libraries become hubs for all kinds of exciting media activities, they needn't always be bookish either.

We agree with David Lankes (2012) that the mission of today's public library should be to facilitate knowledge creation. We aim to inspire and support the general public with access to media of all kinds. For us, the library is a place where people come to learn about any subject that may interest them. Unlike twenty-first-century schools, with their tendency to emphasize passing exams and standardized tests, libraries are spaces where children and young people can come to explore the worlds of culture and media on their own terms.

Current readers' advisory principles encourage us to help users cross the boundaries of genre, author, and medium: today's library collections encompass DVDs, games, music, local studies resources, family history materials, and much more. In the age of participatory pop culture, we believe events involving role-play and gaming are as relevant to libraries' missions as any other item on the shelves.

We've been working together in the Australian town of Parkes, New South Wales, for three years. In everything we do, the aim is to push boundaries in every sense—extending literacy beyond the walls of the library and beyond our usual conceptions of reading, writing, and narrative.

We believe that the best library youth activities:

- draw on existing resources, to conserve budgets;
- engage communities and potential sponsors with a locally relevant narrative; and
- combine storytelling with hands-on challenges and literacy objectives to create memorable learning opportunities.

In this chapter, we discuss:

- converting library spaces into "underground caverns" for a spooky storytelling adventure supported by a local mining firm;
- bringing fathers and babies into the library with an exciting, competitive activity based on decorating boxcar racers;
- activities that blend hands-on craft and literacy for all ages, from real-life games of Angry Birds to werewolf-themed role-playing for teens; and
- a live action zombie siege, covered by the Australian Broadcasting Corporation, in which children and teens found themselves under attack from zombies, forced to research for their lives while barricaded in a tiny rural library.

These case studies and others will illustrate the practical tips in this chapter. Those tips boil down to six easily implemented ideas (discussed in more detail later in the chapter):

- Steal an exciting idea from pop culture.
- Tell a compelling story.
- Provide a hands-on activity.
- Provide a rich language activity.
- Share the kids' work.
- Always make participants join your library—and always make them borrow.

Case Study 1: Mysteries Underground—a Schools Outreach Workshop

Mysteries Underground was a storytelling event for ages eight through twelve. School students on a class visit were told that they were on a mission to explore mysterious caverns that had opened up below their library.

Blacking out windows with masking tape and plastic bags, librarians had decorated the "caverns"—meeting rooms and public spaces—with esoteric items from their homes: everything from cow skulls to wheelbarrows full of coal, plastic skeletons, and even a vast painting of a monster, left over from a Halloween party.

The "tunnel" leading to the cavern was created using tables covered by tarps, which the kids had to crawl under. Wearing hard hats and safety vests provided by a local mining firm, they explored the strange environment before arriving in the cavern, where a librarian told them a story about three children who went into a cave to rescue their cat from a monster.

This was a simple piece of oral storytelling, with lots of repetition and participatory actions to keep the audience engaged and involved. Immediately afterward, the children had time to enjoy a snack and freely explore the environment, wandering through the cavern and discussing the items on display. This provided a rich stimulus for the subsequent writing activity.

After the break, the children had to draw and write a description of an item they would be able to use to defeat the underground monster from the story. They then wrote an illustrated plan of how to use the item against the creature. Children drafted, discussed, and edited their text in pairs before sharing words and pictures with the whole group.

This schools outreach workshop offers an example of our broader attitude to education in libraries. Of course we're pleased if library facilities and homework clubs help students to make their grades and get the best out of their schooling, but we don't see the library as subordinate to the education system. Instead, we're trying to inspire children and young people—to help them see that the library will be their lifelong friend and first port of call whenever they want to explore a new topic or facet of culture and information. As British columnist Caitlin Moran (2012) put it, "A library in the middle of a community is a cross between an emergency exit, a life raft and a festival. They are cathedrals of the mind; hospitals of the soul; theme parks of the imagination."

Our events provoke and inspire the community, at all ages, to recognize this fact about their library. They are "water cooler moments" for kids and teens—compelling experiences that will enrich their lives and keep the library in their hearts and minds for weeks, months, and years to come.

Case Study 2: Rocket Man—Sessions for Fathers and Babies

Fathers' unique style of play and language can provide opportunities for a range of psychological and physical development that is thought to have direct impact on a child's school readiness (Fletcher 2013). Libraries are in the perfect position to respond using recommended best practice and scientific theory—all sneakily packaged inside fun, dynamic activities.

Building on a belief that fathers can play an integral role in their children's early learning, Rocket Man was our attempt to change the way dads think—to encourage them to take their very youngest children to the library, rather than to other free leisure venues like the park.

An informal survey suggested that local dads wanted events outside of normal business hours, and that they found the early literacy programs excessively geared toward mothers. Fair or not, this was a perception on the part of our users that we wanted to challenge.

From inception, Rocket Man was a thirty-minute weekly program targeted toward men and their babies. The main feature of this session was the "boxcar": each father was supplied with a cardboard box big enough to support a child aged twelve months or younger, along with a variety of inexpensive craft items like paper circles, silver pie plates, straws, and colored paper—all for the purpose of custom building their very own rocket car.

With baby safely supported and contained within the car, the dad was free to indulge in special play as librarians delivered a "wriggle and rhyme" session. The rhyme and rhythm of the language provided perfect movement cues. Gentle rocketing across the carpet sparked a myriad of "Brmm, brmms" and "Beep, beeps" that had every baby gurgling. A touch-and-feel board book, a brief interactive story, a few tickles and wiggly toes, and presto! Suddenly Saturday morning at the local library was fueled by a different vibe.

Pilot sessions delivered a few revelations:

- Rocket Man appeals to all age ranges and both sexes.
- Primary-school-aged children have no hang-ups about gate crashing the groups and are happy to take turns squishing into cardboard boxes to sing rhymes and read.
- Dads will swap car stories and share narratives about parenting and playing with children.
- It's okay if a woman runs this "dad-friendly" session.
- Rocket Man is a cheap marketing tool that provokes conversation.

Because of Rocket Man, Parkes Library has now established a link with the Fathers and Families Research Program at the University of Newcastle. Although it was designed by a local librarian to pragmatically meet a local need, Rocket Man's methods reflect contemporary research findings and recommendations (University of Newcastle–Australia 2013), which prompted a member of the university research team to contact the library.

This link has proved valuable and is a source of comfort and inspiration: the university's work confirms the idea that dads do not join standard groups—that services which want to attract and engage fathers long term need to make their groups father specific, active, and wonder based (Fletcher 2013). Curiosity sparks conversation and helps develop literacy, and self-regulation can be learned through rough-and-tumble play—two key areas where fathers have major impacts on early childhood development.

Getting a library noticed brings rewards in all shapes and sizes. Library staff feel validated and encouraged. Governing and funding bodies are delighted!

However, our team members never rest on their laurels and are already looking at future developments, including a "drive-in movie" for the boxcars, a family barbecue for participants, and a "car wash" with local businesses invited to sponsor the event.

Case Study 3: From Video Games to the Living Dead—Holiday Activities for All Ages

The next program arose from Matt's desire to challenge preconceptions about video gaming and literacy. On one hand, video games can be demonized as the nemesis of the book; on the other, there's often a foolhardy rush to requisition iPads and other gadgets as items that will automatically make your library's youth offerings seem cool and relevant.

We believe that youth engagement is as much about respecting the pop-cultural interests of children and young people as it is bringing expensive technology into your sessions. As Jackie Marsh (2000) of Sheffield University has argued:

> Popular culture is, for many children in industrialized societies, a major source of pleasure. Much of children's popular culture is related to the media. Television shows, video games, comics or the latest Disney film provide a plethora of texts with which children become emotionally engaged. (121)

With this in mind, we based an activity for the school vacations on Angry Birds. In this popular video game, the player catapults birds at the pigs' buildings in order to take revenge on the pigs who stole the birds' eggs.

Children entered the library foyer to find Angry Birds decorations on the walls. They decorated their faces with streaks of face paint in the Angry Birds' colors. The video game was projected onto a large screen hooked up to a laptop, and children took turns to play. Children who didn't know the game were shown how to play by their peers.

After a few rounds of Angry Birds, we talked as a group about the pigs and the birds. Are all the pigs evil or just the ones who stole the birds' eggs? Are the birds right to be avenging themselves against every single pig?

The example from our holiday session is very simple, but imagine using Angry Birds as a way to explore conflict resolution. You could even use the game as an unusual opener for more literary discussions: one commentator on our project made a thought-provoking link to that most political of novelists George Orwell (1945) via the final words of *Animal Farm*: "The creatures outside looked from pig to man, and from man to pig, and from pig to man again; but already it was impossible to say which was which" (112).

After the discussion, we challenged the children to build a new Pig City that would resist the Angry Birds' attack. Working in small groups, each child had to design a construction based on the resources available—craft materials and cardboard boxes from local retailers' recycling bins. Each group then chose to build the design they thought would be most robust.

After the design phase, we took a snack break. Children were free to wander around, examining the boxes and each group's designs, before they began construction. Once the buildings were completed, children toured the area, voting for which buildings they thought would best survive the birds' attack. Finally, we put each construction to the test by throwing an Angry Bird toy at it. The buildings were so tough that even the parents we invited into the area were unable to knock them down.

When Matt presented this program at a youth library conference in neighboring New Zealand, we were excited to find that a member of Auckland's library service had run a similar event called Angry Kiwis. It was a great reminder to always share good practice with your colleagues—sometimes the best ideas for youth activities are right under your nose.

Another program, our Fruit Ninja event, was inspired by the popular smart phone game. It's not overburdened with narrative or literacy elements: players slice fruit as it passes across their screens, scoring points for the number of pieces they manage to dice. We added our own story, a riff on *The Magnificent Seven*, about a town besieged by fruit-throwing bandits. The children were invited to enter a "ninja training school" to defend their community.

Drawing on the tradition of Japanese endurance television shows that subject contestants to increasingly ludicrous challenges, we made the trainee ninjas walk stealthily on crinkled-up garbage bags; eat weird food (such as mustard-slathered cakes and wasabi peas in yogurt); and create their own ninja uniform with plastic aprons and crepe-paper bandannas. At the climax of the story, children were invited to play a real-life version of the Fruit Ninja game, smashing and splattering overripe fruit with their bare hands. The children then wrote their own stories about the Fruit Ninja's adventures.

As a holiday activity, our focus was to create a high-energy, tactile experience for under-elevens. This activity can include an emphasis on literacy (writing stories, use of rich vocabulary to describe each fruit before smashing) or healthy eating (discussion of various foodstuffs during practical activities).

These experiences are valid for teens as well as younger children. During the same holiday period, we ran an activity for young people based on the adult fairy tales of Angela Carter. After Matt told teen participants a bleak and bloody version of *Beauty and the Beast*, they decorated blank face masks in the style of a Venetian ball—flamboyant yet ominous. These masks were then used in a simple role-playing activity in which the kids had to question group members to identify two "werewolves" hidden in their midst.

US library technologist and pop culture guru Miguel Rodriguez has argued for the power of horror as a genre that engages children and young people in a library setting. In a piece for *School Library Journal*'s pop-cultural blog *Connect the Pop* (2012), he wrote:

> Despite the general discomfort that seems to arise at the mention of the horror genre—particularly in the fields of education—it clearly offers a unique opportunity for not only engaging young people in reading, but also for sparking the discussion of difficult topics that tend to lurk beneath horror's metaphorical surface.

The success of our werewolf workshop encouraged us to be even more daring when we decided to subject a group of kids and teens to a zombie siege in a rural library. Children across the age range from eight to eighteen years were invited to a school storytelling workshop in the small rural library of Tullamore, only to be barricaded within the building while local volunteers dressed as zombies besieged them. Students had to research survival techniques and plan an escape from the zombie uprising. The local fire service provided support, delivering food crates and guiding the children to a "safe zone" within the school at the end of the day. The immersive role-playing scenario, in which the whole town appeared to have been taken over by zombies and even the real-life emergency services were involved, captured the children's imaginations and attracted additional publicity for the library service. Since the 2012 pilot, this has grown to a two-day event involving students from three schools and a local university, with television coverage from the Australian Broadcasting Corporation (Virtue 2013).

The Principles behind Children's and Youth Activities

Behind each of our case studies lies the same basic structure. It's a framework for inspiration rather than a set of restrictive rules—a process we use to devise activities that engage our readers with a quirky approach to literacy and play.

Here again is the outline:

- Steal an idea.
- Tell a story.
- Provide a hands-on activity.
- Provide a rich language activity.
- Share the kids' work.
- Always make them join; always make them borrow.

Let's look at each of these in more detail.

Steal an Idea

Find some piece of pop culture that will capture the kids' attention. This could be a video game, a book, a song, or a movie—anything from *Captain America* to the "Gangnam Style" pop video. As we discussed earlier, research by Jackie Marsh (2000) backs up what common sense suggests: it's a smart move to address kids through the pop culture materials that they actually consume. We're librarians, not preachers or teachers; we respect and facilitate the cultural interests of all our readers, including the six-year-old fan of *My Little Pony* or *The Amazing Spider-Man*.

Tell a Story

Model good storytelling and give some context to your activities by creating a wider narrative for your workshop. Stories are an engine for engagement: they inspire kids and give both structure and a literacy element to activities like fruit smashing, which might otherwise seem out of place in a library.

Provide a Hands-On Activity

Remember art and craft lessons at school? Often, as you worked, teachers would give you time for your mind to wander or for you to chat with your friends as you carefully worked to create an object or artwork. This time encourages children to act independently and confidently within the group.

As long as your hands-on activity ties in to a wider literacy objective, this can be only a good thing for the library. It's all too easy for libraries to deliver "glitter-and-glue" craft activities with limited literacy value. If we spend time making and decorating a mask in our sessions, we make sure it's then employed in a game or role-playing activity. Don't be afraid to break out the scissors and sticker paper, but make sure that they're used to enhance literacy or library skills and to promote stories in all their forms.

Provide a Rich Language Activity

The need for literacy objectives leads us to rich language activities. Perhaps in your session you'll have the children write a story, poem, or nonfiction text. Don't forget that speaking and listening are valid and meaningful, too—literacy covers everything from debates and discussions to joke telling and board games.

Not every literacy activity involves marks on a page: remember that schools assess speaking and listening skills in their students, and that UNESCO (United Nations Educational, Scientific and Cultural Organization) works to preserve intangible heritage such as dance and oral traditions. If it's good enough for the United Nations, surely it's fair game for librarians, too.

Share the Kids' Work

Always give participants the chance to take pride in their work and share it with their friends, peers, and parents. This could mean anything from show-and-tell time at the end of a workshop to a full gallery display within your library.

Always Make Them Join; Always Make Them Borrow

How daring are you in your pursuit of new readers? We're only half joking when we say that no child leaves one of our workshops without signing up for a library card and taking out at least two books. It might not guarantee repeat business, but as long as it's done with a sense of humor, this kind of attitude can help ensure that your workshop attendees become committed library users.

Don't draw the line at the examples we've given in this chapter. We've also used this approach to create time travel role-playing games and live action Godzilla-versus-robot battles (Library as Incubator Project 2014). This simple structure can be used for anything from an archaeology workshop to forensic science or simple storytelling.

REFERENCES

Fletcher, Richard. 2013. "The Fathers for School Readiness Project." Paper presented at the Australian Research Alliance for Children and Youth Webinar, Newcastle, New South Wales, Australia, October 18.

Lankes, R. David. 2012. *Expect More: Demanding Better Libraries for Today's Complex World*. N.p.: CreateSpace Independent Publishing Platform.

Library as Incubator Project. 2014. Pages tagged 'Matt Finch.' *Library as Incubator Project* (blog), April 5. www.libraryasincubatorproject.org/?s=matt+finch.

Marsh, Jackie. 2000. "Teletubby Tales: Popular Culture in the Early Years Language and Literacy Curriculum." *Contemporary Issues in Early Childhood* 1: 119–33.

Moran, Caitlin. 2012. "Libraries: Cathedrals of Our Souls." *Huffington Post*, September 11. www.huffingtonpost.com/caitlin-moran/libraries-cathedrals-of-o_b_2103362.html.

Orwell, George. 1945. *Animal Farm*. London, UK: Secker and Warburg.

Rodriguez, Miguel. 2012. "How I Learned to Stop Worrying and Love the Monster: Overcoming the Stigma of the Horror Genre." *Connect the Pop* (blog), October 29. http://blogs.slj.com/connect-the-pop/2012/10/movies/guest-post-by-miguel-rodriguez-how-i-learned-to-stop-worrying-and-love-the-monster-overcoming-the-stigma-of-the-horror-genre.

University of Newcastle–Australia. 2013. "Dads Reading to Their Bubs." *Fatherhood Research Bulletin* 16: 8. www.newcastle.edu.au/__data/assets/pdf_file/0006/43818/FRB-Vol-16-JAN-2013.pdf.

Virtue, Robert. 2013. "'Zombies' Invade Western NSW." Australian Broadcasting Corporation. Posted October 14. www.abc.net.au/local/videos/2013/10/14/3868601.htm.

15

•••‒‒••

Librari-Con

Bringing Magic to Your Library

Erika Earp and Melissa Lang

Librari-Con at Cumberland County Public Library & Information Center (CCPL&IC), in Fayetteville, North Carolina, began several years ago when two teen-serving staff decided to create a free comic convention for teens in Cumberland County, North Carolina. There are several large, commercial conventions that teens in our area would talk about wanting to attend, but the lack of transportation and the cost of the tickets, travel, and possibly staying in a hotel were prohibitive. They desperately wanted to geek out with other teens who loved the same shows and series, but the reality was that many of them simply could not afford to participate. Thus, Librari-Con came into being as a free, family-friendly, day-long event to celebrate anime and manga (Japanese animation and comics) and science fiction for teens in our area. Over the years it has grown substantially in popularity. Planning is now year-round, as opposed to that crazy first year when everything was organized in two months. There are now several staff members and community volunteers on a committee who meet in February to plan the essentials: picking a date, discussing the budget, brainstorming possible programs and identifying potential speakers, finding an artist for the mascot, updating the forms and applications, attracting artists to participate, soliciting donations, and providing for safety and security.

Librari-Con came from humble beginnings. That first year, librarian Melissa Lang could afford to spend fifty dollars from teen programming funds, and that just paid for food to feed the volunteers. Library Associate

Katharine Rankin had contacts with local anime clubs who became a great source for community volunteers and networking. In addition, Rankin was on staff at a professional convention in Raleigh called Animazement. She took that opportunity to invite artists there to participate in our convention. Similarly, Lang regularly attended Heroes-Con in Charlotte, North Carolina. She looked for artists who lived near Fayetteville and asked them if they'd like to participate.

Teen Services receives a yearly allotment from our Friends of the Library group that funds programs and refreshments. Librari-Con is paid for by the Friends, and as Librari-Con has grown, staff has asked for and received a larger budget. In 2013, the budget increased to 500 dollars to do the following: purchase tablecloths, craft supplies for the children's area, wristbands, lanyards, food for staff and volunteers, and office supplies, and pay the fee to close the street directly in front of the Headquarters Library for the day. Not included in the budget are printing costs for signs, posters, convention brochures, and official name tags for staff, volunteers, Artist Alley participants, and speakers. The library's Community Relations department pays for this out of a separate fund and allocates about 300 dollars annually from county funds to provide these marketing materials.

To staff Librari-Con, we rely on library workers, community volunteers, and our teen volunteers, whom we lovingly refer to as Minions. The first Minions were teens who regularly attended library programs, including the anime club, and who were excited to finally have "their own convention." Many people have been volunteering since Librari-Con began, and several of our Minions have returned after graduation from high school to continue helping with the event. To find out who can assist, each year we send out an e-mail about two months before the event, asking for help from both the staff and our pool of previous volunteer workers.

The Headquarters Library, where Librari-Con is held, always has one armed security guard on duty. Library administration hires a second security guard for our event to make sure all patrons are safe and supervised. Most incidents have involved reinforcing existing library rules, and this allows library staff to focus on running the programs and helping visitors rather than enforcement. A safety issue particular to our location is the street directly in front of the building. For two years, traffic was allowed to function normally during the convention; however, there has always been a concern about pedestrians in the crosswalk. Cars were not yielding for teens crossing the street, and the teenagers, being excited and incautious, would frequently dart out or chase one another into the street. Library staff investigated options, and we now apply for a block party permit every year to close off a section of the street to traffic, ensuring everyone's safety. It is an extra cost, but well worth the safety it ensures.

In the planning stage, a committee discusses what worked well the previous year (e.g., anime karaoke was really popular) and what didn't (e.g., having anime karaoke outside was a disaster because it was extremely hot). We decide what programs will work in which conference rooms or forum areas. If someone suggests a panel on Japanese culture or language, the immediate question is, who can we get to present that? CCPL&IC is fortunate to have two universities and a college nearby to ask for presenters; however, speakers have also come from the community, local high schools, and other library staff. We often find out that staff members have special interests or skills if we simply ask.

The terms *panel* and *forum* are often used interchangeably, but there is a slight difference. Panels usually involve two or more people speaking about a topic or giving a demonstration. Forums are usually led by an individual, and the audience often participates. Librari-Con asks staff members and community volunteers to come up with ideas and present or to seek out particular speakers on different topics. The organizers also allow convention-goers to propose and run a panel or forum. Interested parties must submit an application with a presenter, backup presenter, topic, and any audiovisual (AV) needs (see figure 15.1). E-mail or phone communication between the applicant and one of the committee members helps to sort out any issues of copyright or appropriateness. For example, a panel on creating "fan subs" for which one edits anime and music together to make a music video was not allowed because of the overwhelming potential for copyright infringement.

Even though Librari-Con is primarily aimed at teenagers, we make sure to include activities for all ages. The Children's Department becomes Chibi Corner. (*Chibi* is Japanese slang for short person or small child.) Chibi Corner features activities like coloring, making superhero capes and masks, and origami. We also offer programs for adults. Snow Wildsmith, author of *A Parent's Guide to the Best Kids' Comics*, has presented programs for parents and teachers about graphic novels. The Cosplay (costume play) Runway is an

Application for Forum, Panel, or Activity

Librari-Con 2013
Cumberland County Public Library & Information Center
Headquarters Library • 300 Maiden Lane • Fayetteville, NC 28301
Saturday, August 31, 2013, from 10:00 a.m.–5:00 p.m.

Name of group: _____

Primary group contact: _____

(Contact must be 18 or older)

Secondary contact: _____

Group mailing address: _____

_____

Phone: _____ E-mail: _____

Group website (to be posted on the Librari-Con website):

_____

Title of event: _____

Name(s) of presenter(s): _____

Backup presenter (required): _____

Backup presenter's contact information: _____

What size room do you need? Please check one.

_____ Conference Room (12–15 people)
_____ Commons Area (25–50 people)
_____ Digital Arts Lab (15–20 people)

Please describe your forum, panel, or activity in detail. This description will be used in the printed Librari-Con program and on the Librari-Con website.

(continued on next page)

FIGURE 15.1
Application for Forum, Panel, or Activity

(continued from previous page)

_____

_____

_____

Please list any special equipment needed for your presentation.

_____

_____

_____

_____   _____
(Signature of presenter)   (Date)

Please mail the completed form to:

> Melissa Lang, Assistant Youth Services Coordinator,
> Cumberland County Public Library & Information Center,
> 300 Maiden Lane, Fayetteville, NC 28301

Panel and forum space will not be assigned until the signed form is received by the Cumberland County Public Library and the panel, forum, or activity is approved.

activity that all ages can participate in and show off their fun costumes. They sign up throughout the day and then the runway show is in the afternoon.

CCPL&IC has an anime license for shows licensed by FUNimation; the license price is based on population and is around 500 dollars for us. If a title that we want to show isn't included in the license, library staff e-mail or call the company that owns it and ask for permission to show the particular episode or movie. As long as we provide a date and time and explain the scope of the event (e.g., whether or not admission is being charged), companies usually give permission to show their titles for free. However, we found that sometimes companies go out of business and often a US company hasn't picked up the rights. When this happens, we make every effort to get viewing permissions. Librari-Con treats all permissions as a donation and credits companies on the event website, on our social media outlets, and in the convention brochure.

Librari-Con promotion takes a county-wide effort. The library has several free media outlets that we utilize: community television, a county public relations department, a column in the local newspaper, Facebook, Twitter, Flickr, and word of mouth. We also post our event on aggregate sites that list comic/anime conventions so that fans from around the state can find out about our convention. Word gets around really fast when people realize the event is free. The library also prints out fliers, posters, and signs to distribute to local schools and throughout the community. Librari-Con also is listed on the Fayetteville Convention and Visitor's Bureau's calendar of events. We even make screen savers that advertise the program for our catalog computers, and library staff wear special buttons the month prior to Librari-Con.

Another feature that makes our convention interesting is that we write to local and national companies asking for donations to give to attendees at our Freebies Table. Most often, we ask for and receive bookmarks, comic books, posters, and postcards with artwork from movies, television shows, and popular comics. Some companies have sent us toys, pins, and buttons. We tailor our requests to each company; for example, if it's a publisher, we ask for something that promotes the company's latest release, and if a PR firm for a movie, we ask for posters or bookmarks. In each request, we give the companies an estimate of the number of event attendees and assure them that we will not be reselling any items they donate. CCPL&IC thanks companies who donate to Librari-Con by mentioning them on our convention webpage (with a link to their website), on our Facebook and Twitter accounts, and in the printed convention brochure.

From the start, Librari-Con reached out to local anime clubs and community groups to help run the convention and to make the programs more authentic. The East Coast Anime Society and Anime Arsenal, a team of artists, were both very helpful; they provided expert advice about how to run a convention and explained what participants would expect, and they also provided speakers and presenters for such forums as "playing tabletop role-playing games," "how to draw manga," and "publishing your own comic book." The Society for the Refinement of Polyvarietal Entertainment (an anime club from North Carolina State University) has sent members for several years to run the anime viewing room and gaming activities.

Often at conventions, people will adorn their outfits with authentic weaponry. However, bringing a weapon into the library is against the rules, so we have to be very specific about the weapons policy (see figure 15.2). We do not allow metal weapons of any kind, including swords, *shurikens* (concealed throwing weapons), or *kunai* (daggers). Weapons that shoot projectiles, like crossbows, air guns, or replica guns, are also prohibited. Props that

Costumes, Props, and Weapons Policy

The Cumberland County Public Library & Information Center wants to create a safe environment for all attendees, while also allowing costumers to show off their hard work and craftsmanship. Please review this page to ensure your costumes and props follow Librari-Con guidelines. Failure to adhere to this policy can result in immediate expulsion from the Library and the convention. Shoes must be worn at all times.

Forbidden Costumes and Props

Items that are <u>strictly prohibited include:</u>

- Metal weapons—including swords, knives, shurikens, kunai, etc.
- Guns—anything that shoots a projectile or could be enabled to shoot a projectile, including air guns, airsoft weapons, crossbows, Nerf weapons, or replicas of actual guns.
- Signs—including all message-based signs attached to costumes, picket signs, polling signs, and dry-erase boards, unless authorized by the Library.

2013 Update

There will be a peace-bonding station outside the main entrance of the Library.

(continued on next page)

FIGURE 15.2
Costumes, Props, and Weapons Policy

(continued from previous page)

All weapon props and staffs or walking sticks must be bonded with a zip tie or fluorescent tape before entering the building.

Realistic toy guns, even those which are not capable of firing a projectile, must be clearly marked at all times so that police officers and other security personnel do not mistake them as real weapons.

Restricted Props and Costumes

Items that <u>are permitted with certain limitations include:</u>

- Easily identifiable toy plastic guns.
- Wooden bokkens, staffs, or walking sticks.
- Fake weapons made from cardboard, Styrofoam, rubber, or other craft materials.

Misusing a prop, or engaging in horseplay by swinging it around, sparring, etc., is the fastest way to lose the privilege of carrying it at all.

You may be asked by the Library staff or the convention staff to remove a prop. If this happens, you must cease wearing it and remove it from the convention area immediately. All props are subject to review by the Library and convention staff.

Costume Guidelines

Librari-Con is a family-friendly convention. All costumes worn at the convention should be suitable for public display. We reserve the right to insist on modifications to costumes. Shoes must be worn at all times.

Due to space limitations and safety issues, large costumes and large props will not be permitted in Artist Alley/Pate Room.

are allowed include easily identifiable toy guns, *bokkens* (wooden training swords), staffs, and fake weapons made out of materials like Styrofoam or cardboard. Starting in 2013, a peace-bonding station was added outside the library's main entrance to inspect all props. With nearly 1,000 in attendance in 2012, it was difficult for staff to keep an eye out for weapons, so we decided that adding a weapons check outside would create a safer environment. This also makes it easier for library security guards, police officers, or sheriff's deputies on duty at the convention to know that a weapon is fake. If anyone misuses a prop, sparring with another attendee or swinging it around, the person will be asked to remove the prop from the library.

Because Librari-Con is a family-friendly convention, all costumes worn at the convention need to be suitable for public display. "Suitable for public display" means the costume covers the same area a swimsuit would cover, plus six inches. There has been the occasional questionable costume over the years, but most participants follow our guidelines. We reserve the right to insist on modifications to costumes, and shoes must be worn at all times.

The Artist Alley is the place for artists to sell their work and sign autographs, and because it is incredibly popular, we put this feature in our biggest meeting room. Artists from North Carolina and South Carolina register for either a half (three feet) or a full (six feet) table in the room to sell original art or craft items. At professional conventions, artists generally pay a "table fee" to participate in an Artist Alley; since ours is in a public library, there are different rules. Unlike professional conventions, official, licensed merchandise cannot be sold. When they register for a table, artists provide a list of the items that they plan to sell. Our Friends group has a form that must be signed saying the artists agree to donate 20 percent of their proceeds to the Friends, who then provide the funds for future Youth Services programs, including the budget for events like Librari-Con. This agreement is standard for anyone selling anything on library property and was established by the Library Trustees (see figure 15.3). In addition, the Friends have a table in the Artist Alley where they sell donated and gently used graphic novels, manga, and anime. The library also has a table in the room for a staff member who helps the artists and provides information for the attendees. The artists are allowed in the day before the convention and two hours before it starts to set up their tables. As our event has grown, artists have begun contacting us early, and the Artist Alley typically fills up less than a month after the application is made available online (see figure 15.4).

Since visitors tend to walk in and out of the building over the course of the day, it's not easy to get an accurate count of attendees. We buy a specific number of wristbands and put one on every attendee as they enter. At the end of the day, we count how many we have left and subtract this amount from the original number to determine attendance at the event. We also

Memorandum of Agreement

Friends of the Cumberland County
Public Library & Information Center, Inc.
Memorandum of Agreement

I, (full name of contact) _____

of (full name of group) _____,

am scheduled to appear at the Cumberland County Public Library & Information Center's Headquarters Library, 300 Maiden Lane, Fayetteville, NC, on Saturday, August 31, 2013, for Librari-Con 2013 Artist Alley.

I will donate 20 percent of any proceeds I receive from the sale of my/our

_____

(Book, CD, DVD, or art)

to the Friends of the Cumberland County Public Library & Information Center, Inc.

_____   _____

(Signature of participant)   (Date)

- -

(For office use only)

_____   _____

(Signature of program coordinator)   (Date)

Coordinator: Send a copy of this memo to the Marketing and Communications Manager prior to the program. Fill out the bottom portion after the event and send the completed form along with the donation you receive from the presenter to the Administrative Assistant to the Director.

Total Sales: _____
Friends' 20 percent: _____
Coordinator's initials: _____

FIGURE 15.3
Memorandum of Agreement

Artist Alley Registration

Librari-Con 2013
Cumberland County Public Library & Information Center
Headquarters Library • 300 Maiden Lane • Fayetteville, NC • 28301
Saturday, August 31, 2013 from 10:00 a.m.–5:00 p.m.

Studio name: _____

Contact: _____
(Contact must be 18 or older)

Secondary contact: _____

Studio address: _____

_____

Phone: _____ E-mail: _____

Studio website (to be posted on the Librari-Con website):

_____

Please choose one.

_____ ½ table (3 ft, maximum one artist—one badge issued)
_____ full table (6 ft, maximum three artists—two badges issued)

Please list the names of all persons authorized to sell at your table. You must be 18 or older to sell at the Librari-Con Artist Alley.

_____

_____

- Please attach a complete and detailed list of all items to be sold, along with their estimated prices. Only original art or crafts that you have created, or that pertain to your work, studio, and/or club, may be sold at Librari-Con.

(continued on next page)

FIGURE 15.4
Artist Alley Registration

(continued from previous page)

- There is a maximum of one person per half table and two persons per full table permitted behind each table at all times during Librari-Con.
- Set up for Librari-Con 2013's Artist Alley is available from 10:00 a.m.–5:30 p.m. on Friday, August 30, and from 8:00 a.m.–10:00 a.m. on Saturday, August 31.

Please check below if:

_____ Space for a backdrop display is needed.
_____ Electrical outlet is needed.

I have read both the registration and agreement forms and agree to the terms therein.

_____   _____
(Authorized signature—signer must be 18 or older)   (Date)

Please mail both completed forms to:

Melissa Lang, Assistant Youth Services Coordinator,
Cumberland County Public Library & Information Center,
300 Maiden Lane, Fayetteville, NC 28301

Tables in Artist Alley will not be reserved or assigned until both completed and signed forms are received and accepted by the Cumberland County Public Library.

keep track of how many people come into the Artist Alley and attend panels and forums. Over the past seven years, event attendance has steadily risen from around 200 to almost 1,300.

In our three-story building, communication can be difficult. In previous years, staff members used cell phones to check in and to ask questions. This works, however, only if the person being called hears the phone ring, and if the caller actually dials a staff member's cell phone and not the person's home phone, which has happened. Ultimately, we decided to increase our budget to buy walkie-talkies. Another advantage that helps immensely during the convention is our legion of Minions. They assist staff members with whatever we may need. Mostly this includes such tasks as "Can you find Keith and ask him where the extension cord is?" and "Please find Vicki and ask if she needs help with crafts."

The day before the convention, we begin setting up for the event. The maintenance staff transforms some of the areas of the library into forum areas, sets up chairs in the storytime room for anime viewing, and moves the furniture in the Children's Department to make room for crafts and activities. Staff gather all the materials that will be given away during the convention, such as brochures, freebies donated by various companies, and handouts for forums. A library staff member puts together a display of graphic novels and manga. Our marketing department prints all of the posters and signage we need ahead of time, and these are put out the night before. We get all of the screens and projectors prestaged for the next morning. A staff member makes the work schedule for the next day so everyone knows where they are supposed to be and when they get a lunch break. Librari-Con has approximately five community volunteers (the number varies each year) and twenty-two staff (out of over 200) members. Some of the staff work all day, and some work half the day.

The morning of the convention the Artist Alley opens early so the artists can get their name tags and set up their tables. Our convention headquarters, located in one of our conference rooms, opens so that staff, volunteers, guest speakers, and Minions can get their name tags and see the work schedule. The information table in the lobby is stocked with wristbands and convention brochures to hand out to the attendees. Chibi Corner is set up with craft supplies. A computer services staff member sets up laptops for presenters and at the library table in the Artist Alley. One staff member is in charge of preparing the break room. Once the library opens at 9:00 a.m., staff begin putting wristbands on attendees and checking props at the peace-bonding station. The Artist Alley opens and the programs start at 10:00 a.m. During the day, library staff take pictures for the library's Flickr page of all the great events, including the very popular Cosplay Runway, where people can show off their elaborate costumes. We also use various social media sites to make announcements and post pictures, videos, and funny comments. Minions walk around with whiteboards to make announcements. At the end of the day, we hold a closing ceremony to thank the volunteers and staff who make

Librari-Con possible. Then the staff, volunteers, and Minions put the library back together and clean up before finally going home.

There are several housekeeping items to address after the convention. An evaluation survey is posted on our website and social media outlets as soon as possible, either during or directly after the convention ends. We announce during the closing ceremony where participants can find the survey and that suggestions will help make the next year's program even better. During the week after the convention, we collect and process photos taken during the convention. We have found that many participants get their galleries together quickly and begin sharing them online in anime forums and on Facebook, but they are still impatient for the library's official gallery. Staff contact information is posted in case parents or guardians wish to have their teenagers' pictures removed. CCPL&IC operates on verbal consent of an individual to have pictures taken, and requests not to be pictured or filmed are respected.

Finally, the proceeds are gathered from Artist Alley and the Friends book sale. Librari-Con keeps audit sheets and secures all money until it is delivered to library administration. The final tally of the Artist Alley money as well as overall statistics are reported to the library director for the monthly report.

Over the years, we have learned that the best way for us to run Librari-Con is to organize a committee. It takes the pressure of having to do everything off of one or two people. Having a committee makes it easier to assign specific tasks to specific people; we have one person in charge of the Artist Alley, two people in charge of making T-shirts for volunteers, and one person who oversees everything. We also take suggestions from teens who have attended in previous years. Getting responses like "I had a ton of fun!," "Had a very fun time! Can't wait till next year!," and "I finally get to cosplay without traveling far!" from the attendees makes all the hard work worth it. Librari-Con will always be here for the teens who need a free, safe place to make friends and geek out.

This is just our experience with producing a convention in a library. Portions may be scaled down to fit any budget or space. Start small with a few local artists and a panel or two. Let the teens participate. Build your network of contacts and grow a little bit each year. Your teens will appreciate it.

16

· · ◦ ◦ ◦ ◦ ◦

The Business of Ideas

Using a TED-Like Event to Spread Innovation

Troy A. Swanson

In the summer of 2011, I was part of a conversation with the Moraine Valley Community College's Staff Development Specialist from our Center for Teaching and Learning. Our discussion focused on the amazing faculty and staff who work at our college. We agreed that our colleagues were dedicated to their jobs, intellectually engaged in the world around them, and fascinating individuals. We tried to imagine ways that we could encourage our staff members to get to know one another. Our initial concern centered on sharing ideas within the organization. People across departments and divisions may not know one another, even if they share similar interests and work on related projects. How could we reach across organizational boundaries to share ideas in meaningful ways?

The Center for Teaching and Learning (CTL) already hosted many workshops and similar events where staff and faculty shared ideas. In addition, the college hosted two, day-long in-service days that were all-staff learning events. But we recognized the limitations of these opportunities, including a significant investment from the college in staff time and closing all services for a day and inflexible scheduling. We were interested in finding a way to connect people that more easily fit into the daily work of the college. We needed something that was short and digestible that allowed college staff to learn about a colleague and follow up later if needed. Our primary goals, although undocumented at first, were to share ideas within the organization and connect individuals across college divisions. At the time, we joked about asking the organizers of the TED Talks (www.ted.com) to come to our campus and host an event made up just of our staff. This conversation evolved, and after several meetings, we had set a path for something new.

The TLC: Teaching and Learning Center event was openly adapted from the TED Talks. The TED movement has had a significant impact around the world in sharing ideas. Begun in 1984 as a conference focused on technology, entertainment, and design, TED is an annual conference held yearly as a forum for thinkers from around the world to give short talks that are recorded and made available for free. In the fall of 2012, TED reached its billionth video view (TED 2012). Since its inception, TED has expanded from a single event to locally organized events that grow and spread ideas globally and locally.

We recognized the value in the TED model, which transforms a face-to-face event into an online document that can be shared so that conversations continue. We knew that many people on our campus were familiar with the model, so we openly borrowed the look and feel. The simple, storytelling tone makes complicated ideas approachable, and the posting of free videos helps to disseminate ideas globally.

With the TED model in mind, we recognized that TLC could be something with impact beyond our primary goal of idea sharing within the organization. Like other events held in our library, this could be a way to enrich the curriculum and simultaneously reach out to the broader community beyond our main campus. We saw a secondary goal of showing off the talented individuals with whom we worked.

The Space We Occupy

My colleagues and I at Moraine Valley Community College Library have always made it our mission to be more than a storehouse of information or just a study space with computer access. We see our primary business as connecting our students and our larger community to ideas.

We have long recognized that the library fills an important space, both physically and conceptually, within our college community. As a physical space, we are the only open academic space on campus. There are other spaces where academic activities occur, such as theaters, tutoring centers, or classrooms, or markedly nonacademic spaces, such as the college union, but they are not easily accessible to passing students. As a conceptual space, we are one of the few departments that connect the academic with the nonacademic. We host meetings, gatherings, lectures, panel discussions, and films. Some of these events are quite academic, organized by academic departments, and others are nonacademic, organized by student clubs or Student Life. All of these events are advertised to the larger community, and as a result, members of the community often are part of the audience. As a result of our programming efforts, I have often found myself in the position of introducing a faculty member to a staff member from a different organizational division. We make it our goal to be the intellectual hub on our campus that connects the classroom, student activities, and the community at large. Our library's focus is always on enhancing and enabling student learning by supporting our curriculum, but we do this by enabling learning to occur outside of the classroom.

Over the past decade, our library earned a reputation for successful public events. We host six to seven events each semester as part of our One Book, One College programming, and then another eight to ten events each semester that are organized by other departments. We host thirty to thirty-five public events each academic year. In 2014, our zombie apocalypse, active-learning game received the ProQuest Innovation in College Librarianship Award from the Association of College and Research Libraries, and it received our campus's Innovation of the Year Award. Part of our success with public events that have an impact across campus is the utilization of digital media to capture, share, and preserve the live event. The library began distributing audio from public events in 2006 and added video in early 2012. The audio is available as a download from our library's website, in iTunes, and through our social networks. The video is hosted on YouTube and embedded in our blogs and our social networks. Over a six-year period, we built an online infrastructure and created the expectation within our college community that the library is a distribution source for sharing conversations on a nonresidential campus. We have posted 111 videos on a wide range of topics. Our most popular videos include a guest lecture about actuarial science by a practicing actuary, a faculty lecture about why the South was destined to lose the US Civil War, and a faculty lecture about surviving a zombie apocalypse.

The library is the central public place for intellectual exchanges on campus. We strive to embody the mission outlined by David Lankes (2011) in *The Atlas of New Librarianship*, "to improve society through facilitating knowledge creation in their communities" (13).

The Goals of TLC

As mentioned, we envisioned TLC as an avenue for sharing ideas within our larger community and established the following goals:

- Find teachers, innovators, and leaders who are able to inspire us with "ideas worth sharing" (appropriating the language from the TED Talks).
- Create a live learning event that is captured and shared via social media within the larger Moraine Valley community.
- Disseminate ideas in support of Moraine Valley Community College's curriculum.
- Foster knowledge sharing among faculty and staff in support of Moraine Valley Community College's strategic priority of continuous improvement.
- Exhibit Moraine Valley's wide variety of knowledge and talent to the external college community.
- Demonstrate the technology and instructional possibilities that are available within the CTL and library through the live event and the social media offerings.

The CTL, which is the library's sister department within the same subdivision of Academic Affairs, has a mission focused on staff and faculty training. For them, the TLC event is a knowledge management program that increases awareness within the organization. The CTL staff utilize the TLC event to build connections between staff and faculty to increase effectiveness. For the library, TLC is a way to create knowledge within the community by fostering the open exchange of ideas. This supports our goal of fostering the exchange of ideas in order to enrich curriculum and improve learning.

For each TLC event, we produce six fifteen-minute videos. The videos are purposefully short so that the content is focused and meaningful. The length also encourages watching and sharing because the videos do not require a long time commitment. The videos also fulfill an archival role, preserving the event for future viewing.

Approvals within the Organization

Before we could move forward with the project, we sought out administrative support. We wrote a proposal that described the project to our administrators, which also turned out to be useful when recruiting our first speakers. Our first step in the approval process was to sit down with our dean, who directed the CTL and the library. We outlined our plan to her and talked through the event, and she took the proposal to the vice president of Academic Affairs.

Overall, the most significant question that administrators asked was, why was this our job? This was an easy question to answer because our goals and purpose statement clearly tied the TLC event back to the mission of the library and the mission of the CTL. We emphasized that, not only was this our job, but we were the only departments within the larger organization that were positioned to do an event like this. After a short discussion, we had a green light from the college administration.

Accidental Community

My counterpart in the CTL and I recruited our first speakers, purposefully reaching out to individuals we knew who had good stories to share. The speakers were excited to be asked to share their stories. We met with this group at the end of the fall semester and outlined the event. Then the speakers used the winter break as an opportunity to write their talks, and upon returning, my co-organizer and I scheduled a practice session. There was concern that the speakers would go over the time limit.

Deciding to hold this practice was a good decision, as most of the speakers talked significantly longer than fifteen minutes. After each talk, the six speakers and the two event organizers provided feedback to the speakers and suggested changes. We mostly discussed ways to focus the talks in order to get them within the time limit. After the practice session, several speakers were concerned about successfully focusing and editing their talks. They felt the pressure of fitting within the time limit and asked if we could schedule another practice session, which we did. After this session, the participants requested another practice session. In all, we ended up scheduling four practice sessions.

During these sessions, the presenters continued to give one another feedback. There was a great deal of laughter and many moments of awe when a presentation really came together. During these practices, a feeling of community evolved. For those of us involved in the event, these stopped being disconnected talks. We noted connections among them, and all of us felt a degree of ownership over each talk and the event as a whole. In some cases, presenters were sharing very personal stories, such as surviving cancer or dealing with being adopted. The participants dealt with one another with grace. They offered support, shed tears, and helped to mold rough drafts into strong pieces.

From the beginning, we set lofty goals for the TLC event. We had hoped to find amazing stories and to highlight those stories for our larger community, but we did not anticipate that the most important aspect of the TLC event would become content development. The time producing and polishing the content is the most important aspect of this event.

The roadblocks of the first session had lasting changes on the process for all future TLC events, and we approached the second planning process much differently. We scheduled five practice sessions from the outset. When we recruited speakers, we made sure they could commit the time to be at the practice sessions. We built the event around the development of content and committed our participants to helping one another prepare for the day of the event. In each case, the participants have come together and shared of themselves. This alone has helped to build connections within the organization, an unintended outcome of the event.

Hosting the Live Event

The actual live event is more complicated than the library's other cultural events, and the day is always a bit chaotic. Along with our normal chair setup, we also set up for a video shoot, which involves more people.

In the library's event space—a dual-use space—our normal theater seating floor plan has a single aisle in the center, and we set up eighty seats on the floor. When not hosting events, the library uses the event space as a lounge area with comfortable chairs, loveseats, and book displays. The furniture in this space is on casters and can be pulled to the perimeter. When the eighty event chairs are combined with the lounge furniture, we have seating capacity for nearly 100 people.

A retractable video screen that comes down from the ceiling is accompanied by a projector and laptop for presentation slides and web access. This space also includes a sound system with speakers in the ceiling. We use a lavalier microphone for the speakers and a handheld, cordless microphone for introductions. A digital MP3 recorder in the sound system is used to record audio for the podcast and to lay over the video during the editing process.

The video is captured with three high-definition (HD) cameras. One camera is a direct, tight shot of the speaker that follows the speaker closely as he or she moves. This is the main shot used in the video. A second camera captures a wide side shot, while a third camera records an even wider shot that includes a large portion of the room. The latter is the only camera that does not require an operator; the other two require a person to follow the speaker. In addition to these cameras, we use the campus's lecture capture system, which embeds presentation slides along with the video. This provides an additional angle and an easier way to incorporate slides into the video edit.

The lighting in the space is sufficient for most events, but when the end goal is to create a well-produced, HD-quality video, the existing lighting is not enough. Our campus photographer sets up two studio lights, including a big box light, that make the speakers' faces more visible.

The first time we held this event, we did three talks in a row, took a short break, and then we held the remaining three talks. This proved to be problematic for instructors who wanted to bring classes to the event and for staff members who wanted to see a particular individual but couldn't stay for the entire event. The problem was that we didn't know when a particular individual would present over the course of the day.

For the second TLC event, we made some changes to better predict when each speaker would talk. We now hold the event over a three-hour period starting at 11:00 a.m. and ending at 2:00 p.m. We schedule two talks for each hour, and we send out the schedule in advance. One speaker will start at the top of hour, give her or his fifteen-minute talk, and answer a few questions from the audience, and then the next speaker proceeds. When the time for introductions and switching microphones is included, two talks take one hour. At the end of this hour, we take a five- or ten-minute break to allow attending classes to leave and new classes to arrive, and then we start again at the top of the next hour. This schedule has allowed more classes to attend.

We primarily promote the live event to faculty members through e-mail. As soon as the schedule is set, we send out an e-mail to all faculty. We also use other internal modes of communication, such as the staff newsletter. In addition, we include information about the event in the student e-mail newsletter. The college's Public Relations department helps us reach out to the external community by writing a press release for local media and also sharing information on the college's website and social media outlets. Each talk averages forty to 100 audience members. This varies based on interest by classes and the community. Our larger audiences are often a result of faculty members bringing classes to the live event.

The Hardware and Editing Process

Unlike regular library lectures available on the web, the editing process for TLC events is much more involved and, like similar projects, a product of the available technology. Our staff in the Center for Teaching and Learning do the video editing. The library staff members manage the TLC website, upload the videos to YouTube, and share the videos with faculty via e-mail.

Each talk starts out as four separate AVCHD files pulled into iMovie and then converted to MOV files. This process can take several hours. Then the MOV files and audio MP3 file are pulled into Adobe Premiere Pro. To simplify editing, we use a product called PluralEyes from Singular Software to synchronize the four video files with the MP3. PluralEyes essentially uses the audio that is embedded in the video as a guide to match up with the MP3 file. Thus, the audio becomes the mechanism to align the timing for the video in the editing process.

Once the files are transferred back to Premiere Pro, they are ready to be edited. The four files are nested so that they can be viewed at the same time. Different shots are pulled together using natural breaks in the speech, references to the slides, or body movements to switch between shots so that there is a natural flow to the finished video. After the four shots are edited together, the file is transferred back into iMovie. From here the opening bumper, closing trailer, and captions are added to the file. The file size is adjusted and the finished product is uploaded to YouTube. Once in YouTube, the video is tagged and a description is added.

Obviously, this process is time-consuming. Many of the hardware elements we use are personal devices brought from home and not equipment purchased by the college. There are software suites and additional pieces of hardware that would save time, but in lieu of fighting the budgetary approval process, we decided to move the project forward. We believe in the goals of the TLC events enough to make this work with whatever resources are available.

Promoting and Cataloging

The first video is edited and released two or three weeks after the event, and it can take up to three months to get all six videos produced and released. The videos could be produced more quickly, but, of course, the video production must be accomplished along with regular job duties. We take advantage of this delay by using the time between videos to promote and give attention to each video.

Once a video is edited and ready for the public, it is uploaded to YouTube. Then we embed this video on the TLC website homepage as the "featured" video. In addition, we take the MP3 file and make it available as a podcast from the library website. The audio can be downloaded from iTunes or directly from the library podcast page. Next, we create a blog post that includes both the embedded video and the link to the audio podcast. The blog's RSS feed connects to Facebook, Twitter, and Google+, so each post automatically feeds content to these social media sites where it can be further shared. After this, we send out an e-mail to the faculty as well as include it in the weekly staff news e-mail. Next, we send the video link to faculty or staff who teach classes or organize other projects connected to the video content. Finally, each video is cataloged in the library's catalog and uploaded to OCLC (Online Computer Library Center). Our hope is that the videos will be findable along with similar content in the library collection.

Lessons

We learned several important lessons from the TLC events. From the first event forward, we recognized that TLC is not about hosting an event or creating videos; it is about developing content. Most of the time, the library invites speakers to talk about their expertise or to deliver presentations that are also given in other places. These speakers are often scholars, authors, artists, or religious leaders, and they draw their content from their research, writings, or other work. In contrast, when speakers participate in TLC, we ask them to do something different. They do not have an hour to lecture and cannot wander away from the topic. With the fifteen-minute time limit, there is no room for digression, and the speaker must remain focused. Thus, TLC has evolved into a development process during which speakers come together to help one another develop their ideas.

Second, we learned to listen to the speakers in guiding the event. It was the first participants who helped TLC evolve into an idea development process, and we continue to listen to participants' input as each event moves forward. I often ask a speaker to join TLC with a particular subject in mind, but, frequently, the speaker will ask to do something different. I almost always encourage the speaker to go after this new topic. If the person is feeling compelled to go in a new direction, then how can we hold back the idea?

Third, producing high-quality, edited video is a time-intensive process. This will not be a surprise to anyone who has played with video editing. In this project, we are committed to quality. Producing videos of public events can be quite easy with a camera and a decent sound system. However, video production that involves giving videos a polish, working with large file sizes, and editing from multiple cameras is more complex. Some of these challenges can be overcome by adding staff time and buying the right hardware.

Finally, this event was initiated to strengthen ties with the community we serve by sharing ideas, and unexpectedly, a deeper, stronger community emerged among the participants. This results from the personal stories shared in practice sessions and from the emotional support that participants give one another. Each of them knows that they face the audience together and that they all must contend with the clock. During the live events, the audience cannot truly understand the full process behind the stories. They don't see the connections among the participants and the work they have put in over the hours of practice leading up to these fifteen-minute presentations.

We have some measures of the impact of the TLC videos beyond audience attendance and video view counts. Following each TLC event, one or two faculty members will e-mail to inquire about when a particular talk will be available. Several videos have been used in classes during which a faculty member asks students to watch the video and respond in writing.

I have always felt fortunate to be a librarian and to work in a supportive environment like Moraine Valley Community College. When I interviewed for the job, I told the interviewer that my plan was to build experience and see where the future took me. The interviewer, who would be my boss, told me that people tend to stay at Moraine Valley because it is such a good place. After fourteen years, I am still at Moraine Valley, largely because of the people, and the TLC event is a way to show off the commitment, expertise, and engagement of my colleagues.

Libraries are more than book storehouses and study halls with coffee shops. Libraries are in the knowledge creation and idea business. If ideas are the catalyst for innovation, then creating organizations where ideas spread easily is vital to fostering innovation. This is the role of the Moraine Valley Community College Library. Seeking out speakers, finding uplifting stories, encouraging people to participate, and helping to develop these stories all go beyond building a library collection. We fill an intellectual space that is focused on learning but exists beyond the classroom. Our primary goal for the TLC event was sharing innovations within the organization, but our greatest outcome may be the community that this event fosters.

REFERENCES

Lankes, R. David. 2011. *The Atlas of New Librarianship*. Cambridge, MA: MIT Press.
TED. 2012. "TED Reaches Its Billionth Video View." *TED Blog*, November 13. http://blog.ted.com/2012/11/13/ted-reaches-its-billionth-video-view.

ABOUT THE EDITORS AND CONTRIBUTORS

Dr. Anthony Molaro is Assistant Professor in the MLIS Program at St. Catherine University in St. Paul, Minnesota. He is currently researching makerspaces and learning labs in public libraries. His other research and teaching focus is on public services, management, and leadership. He has written and presented on a variety of library topics. You can read his blog at http://informationactivist.com or follow him on Twitter @infoactivist.

Leah L. White is Head of Popular Materials at the Ela Area Public Library District in Lake Zurich, Illinois, and a member of the Adult Reading Round Table Steering Committee. Leah graduated from Dominican University with her MLIS in 2008 and won the *Library Journal* Movers & Shakers Award in 2012. She enjoys reading comic books, Instagramming pictures of her pets, and spending too much time (and money) in independent bookstores. You can find her on Twitter @leahlibrarian or check out her website at www.leahlwhite.com.

Audrey Barbakoff is Adult Services Manager and Adult Services Librarian at Kitsap Regional Library in Washington.

Robin Bergart is User Experience Librarian at the University of Guelph, Ontario, Canada.

Erica J. Christianson is Assistant Director at the Ela Area Public Library District in Lake Zurich, Illinois.

M. J. D'Elia is Learning and Curriculum Support Librarian at the University of Guelph, Ontario, Canada.

Dr. Pat Duck, now retired, was Director of the Millstein Library at the University of Pittsburgh at Greensburg, Pennsylvania, and Coordinator of Regional University Library System Libraries at the University of Pittsburgh.

Erika Earp is Headquarters Information Services Manager for the Cumberland County Public Library system in North Carolina.

Anna Fillmore brings her creative flare to everything she does as Youth Services Librarian II at the Northbrook Public Library in Illinois.

Matt Finch writes and creates fun things for people to do in public places—see more at www.matthewfinch.me.

Ben Haines is Head of Adult Services at the Forest Park Public Library in Illinois.

Tracy M. Hall was Instructional Services Librarian with University Libraries at Virginia Tech. Hall recently accepted a position as Director of a public library in Alabama.

Monica Harris is Deputy Director at the Schaumburg Township District Library in Illinois.

Sarah Hashemi Scott works in Quick Information and serves on the Library Innovation Team at the Seattle Public Library in Washington.

Amy Holcomb wears many hats as Youth Services Librarian at the Northbrook Public Library in Illinois.

Melissa Lang is Assistant Youth Services Coordinator for the Cumberland County Public Library system in North Carolina.

Edward F. Lener is Associate Director of Collection Management and College Librarian for the Sciences with University Libraries at Virginia Tech.

Purdom Lindblad was College Librarian for the Humanities and Digital Humanities with University Libraries at Virginia Tech. Lindblad is currently Head of Graduate Programs at the University of Virginia Library Scholars' Lab in Charlottesville.

Tracie Mauro is Branch Librarian at Parkes Shire Library, New South Wales, Australia.

Cheryl McGrath is Director of Stonehill College Library at Stonehill College in Easton, Massachusetts.

Heather McNamee is Supervising Librarian at the Wallingford Branch of the Seattle Public Library System in Washington.

Kate Niehoff is Popular Services Librarian at the Schaumburg Township District Library in Illinois.

Kelly Pepo was Acquisitions Services Manager for the Orange County Library System in Orlando, Florida, and is currently Branch Manager at the San Diego Public Library in California.

Daisy Porter-Reynolds is Executive Director at Aurora Public Library in Illinois and before that was Director of Services at Arlington Heights Memorial Library in Illinois.

Lorna E. Rourke is Library Director at St. Jerome's University in Waterloo, Ontario, Canada.

Sarah Strahl is Head of Technical Services at the Ela Area Public Library District in Lake Zurich, Illinois.

Troy A. Swanson is Teaching and Learning Librarian and Department Chair of Library Services at Moraine Valley Community College in Illinois.

Brad Warren is Director of Access Services at Yale University Library in New Haven, Connecticut.

INDEX